Lee's EXCELLENT ENGLISH

Vietnamese Edition

Lee's Books

No unauthorized photocopying

All rights reserved. No part of this publication may be reproduced, stored in a retrieval system, or transmitted, in any form or by any means, without the prior permission in writing of Teacher King's Books.

This book is sold subject to the condition that it shall not, by the way of trade or otherwise, be lent, resold, hired out, or otherwise circulated without the publisher's prior consent in any form of binding or cover than that in which it is published and without a similar condition including this condition being imposed on the subsequent purchaser.

Copyright © 2022 Lee's Books
All rights reserved.

ISBN: 9798847347860

Contents

Lesson 1: My pencil case hộp bút — Page 6

Lesson 2: In the classroom trong lớp học — Page 10

Lesson 3: Colors màu sắc — Page 14

Lesson 4: My family gia đình của tôi — Page 18

Lesson 5: Shapes hình dạng — Page 22

Lesson 6: At the zoo tại chợ trái cây — Page 26

Lesson 7: Jobs công việc — Page 30

Lesson 8: At the fruit market tại chợ trái cây — Page 34

Lesson 9: The body cơ thể — Page 38

Lesson 10: Sports thể thao — Page 42

Lesson 11: Places nơi chốn — Page 46

Lesson 12: Clothes quần áo — Page 50

Lesson 13: School subjects những môn học ở trường — Page 54

Lesson 14: Vegetables rau — Page 58

Lesson 15: At the toy shop tại cửa hàng đồ chơi — Page 62

Lesson 16: In the kitchen trong bếp — Page 66

Lesson 17: Feelings cảm xúc — Page 70

Lesson 18: At the ice cream shop tại cửa hàng kem — Page 74

Lesson 19: The weather thời tiết — Page 78

Lesson 20: In the living room trong phòng khách — Page 82

Lesson 21: Chores việc nhà — Page 86

Lesson 22: Pets vật nuôi — Page 90

Lesson 23: Skills kỹ năng — Page 94

Lesson 24: Meats thịt — Page 98

Lesson 25: Countries quốc gia — Page 102

Lesson 26: Languages ngôn ngữ — Page 106

Lesson 27: In the refrigerator trong tủ lạnh — Page 110

Lesson 28: Desserts món tráng miệng — Page 114

Lesson 29: At school ở trường — Page 118

Lesson 30: Transportation vận chuyển — Page 122

Lesson 31: Fast food thức ăn nhanh — Page 126

Lesson 32: Landscapes phong cảnh — Page 130

Lesson 33: Homework bài tập về nhà — Page 134

Lesson 34: The calendar lịch — Page 138

Lesson 35: Camping cắm trại — Page 142

Lesson 36: Daily life cuộc sống hàng ngày — Page 146

Lesson 37: On the street trên đường — Page 150

Lesson 38: Hobbies sở thích — Page 154

Lesson 39: In the bedroom trong phòng ngủ — Page 158

Lesson 40: More places thêm địa điểm — Page 162

Lesson 41: The face khuôn mặt — Page 166

Lesson 42: Personalities tính cách — Page 170

Lesson 43: Music âm nhạc   Page 174

Lesson 44: Activities hoạt động   Page 178

Lesson 45: Outdoor activities các hoạt động ngoài trời   Page 182

Lesson 46: Ocean life thế giới đại dương   Page 186

Lesson 47: In the bathroom trong nhà tắm   Page 190

Lesson 48: Capital cities thành phố thủ đô   Page 194

Lesson 49: In the toolbox trong hộp công cụ   Page 198

Lesson 50: At the cinema ở rạp chiếu phim   Page 202

Answers   Page 206

Lesson 1: My pencil case

hộp bút

Learn the words

1. pencil
   bút chì
2. eraser
   cục gôm
3. glue
   keo dán
4. pencil sharpener
   gọt bút chì
5. whiteout
   bút tẩy

6. pen
   bút mực
7. ruler
   thước
8. tape
   băng keo
9. marker
   bút ghi đậm
10. crayon
    bút sáp màu

Q&A Pattern 1

Where did you buy the pencil case?
I bought it at the supermarket.

Q&A Pattern 2

What do you have in your pencil case?
I have some pencils. I also have a red marker.

Q&A Pattern 3

Do you have any glue?
No, I don't. I have some tape.

Conversation 1

Lucy: I like your new pencil case!

Scott: Thank you. I bought it yesterday.

Lucy: Where did you buy the pencil case?

Scott: I bought it at the supermarket.

Lucy: What do you have in your pencil case?

Scott: I have some <u>pencils</u>. I also have a red <u>marker</u>.

Lucy: Do you have any <u>glue</u>?

Scott: No, I don't. I have some <u>tape</u>.

Lucy: That's good. Can I borrow your <u>tape</u>?

Scott: Yes, you can. Here you are.

Answer the questions

1. What did Scott buy yesterday?

2. Where did he buy the pencil case?

3. Does Scott have any crayons in his pencil case?

4. What does Lucy want to borrow of Scott?

True or False?

1. Scott has a new pencil case.   ☐ **True** ☐ **False**

2. Lucy bought the pencil case at the supermarket.   ☐ **True** ☐ **False**

3. Scott doesn't have any tape.   ☐ **True** ☐ **False**

4. Scott has some pencils and a red marker in his pencil case.   ☐ **True** ☐ **False**

Conversation 2

Scott: I can't find my eraser!

Lucy: What color is it?

Scott: It's a blue and white one. Have you seen it?

Lucy: No, I haven't. When did you use it last?

Scott: I used it in English class this morning.

Lucy: That's strange. I also lost my ruler in English class.

Scott: What color is the ruler?

Lucy: It's the same color as your pencil sharpener.

Scott: I saw Andy using a yellow ruler in English class this morning.

Lucy: I also saw him using a blue and white eraser!

Answer the questions

1. What can't Scott find?
2. When did Scott use his eraser last?
3. What color is Lucy's ruler?
4. Who was using Lucy and Scott's things?

Write the nouns

1. Scott can't find his _____ .
2. Scott was using his eraser in English _____ this morning.
3. Lucy's ruler and Scott's _____ sharpener are the same color.
4. Lucy's _____ is yellow.

Take the test

Write the answer next to the letter "A"

A: ___ **1.** Lucy ___ Scott's new pencil case.

a. like   b. likes   c. liking

A: ___ **2.** Scott bought the pencil case at the ___.

a. supermarket   b. bookstore   c. school

A: ___ **3.** Scott has pencils and a red ___ in his pencil case.

a. crayon   b. pen   c. marker

A: ___ **4.** Lucy borrowed Scott's ___.

a. tape   b. marker   c. glue

A: ___ **5.** Scott cannot find his ___.

a. ruler   b. tape   c. eraser

A: ___ **6.** Scott used the eraser in ___ class.

a. math   b. English   c. science

A: ___ **7.** The color of Lucy's ruler is ___.

a. blue and white   b. red   c. yellow

A: ___ **8.** ___ was using a ruler and an eraser this morning.

a. Andy   b. Lucy   c. Scott

Answers on Page 206

Lesson 2: In the classroom

trong lớp học

Learn the words

1. chair — ghế
2. desk — bàn
3. blackboard — bảng đen
4. whiteboard — bảng trắng
5. computer — máy vi tính
6. globe — quả địa cầu
7. clock — đồng hồ
8. book — sách
9. bookshelf — giá sách
10. poster — áp phích

Q&A Pattern 1

What do you think of our new classroom?
I think it needs a <u>whiteboard</u>.

Q&A Pattern 2

How big are the <u>chairs</u>?
The <u>chairs</u> are the same size as our old ones.

Q&A Pattern 3

Which one is your <u>desk</u>?
It's the one with the blue <u>computer</u> on it.

Conversation 1

Peter: What do you think of our new classroom?

Helen: I think it needs a whiteboard.

Peter: The new blackboard is much bigger than the old one.

Helen: That's true. How big are the new chairs?

Peter: The chairs are the same size as our old ones.

Helen: That's too bad. I think the old ones are too small!

Peter: It sounds like you're not happy about the new classroom.

Helen: There is one thing I like. The bookshelf has many more books.

Peter: I noticed that, too. Are there any books that you haven't read yet?

Helen: Yes, there are many that I still haven't read.

Answer the questions

1. What does Helen think the classroom needs?
2. Is the new blackboard bigger than the old one?
3. Why doesn't Helen like the chairs?
4. What does Helen like about the new classroom?

Complete the sentences using three words

1. Helen thinks the classroom _____.
2. The new blackboard is bigger than _____.
3. Helen thinks the old chairs _____.
4. The bookshelf has _____.

Conversation 2

Helen: I'm glad I can sit next to the window this year.

Peter: You're lucky. I have to sit at the front of the classroom.

Helen: Which one is your desk?

Peter: It's the one with the blue computer on it.

Helen: I still haven't got one. I'll be getting one this weekend.

Peter: I saw a poster with computers on sale at the department store.

Helen: Dad told me about that. I want one like yours.

Peter: It's a good computer. Mom wants to get me a new clock.

Helen: What's wrong with the one you have now?

Peter: It doesn't have an alarm on it. I always wake up too late.

Answer the questions

1. Where does Peter have to sit this year?
2. What color is Peter's computer?
3. When is Helen going to get a computer?
4. Why does Peter's Mom want to get a new clock for him?

Which person?

1. _____ can sit next to the window this year.
2. _____ sits at the desk with the blue computer.
3. _____ told Helen about the computers at the department store.
4. _____ wants to get Peter a new clock.

Take the test

Write the answer next to the letter "A"

A: ___ **1.** Helen thinks the classroom needs a ___.

a. globe					b. blackboard					c. whiteboard

A: ___ **2.** The new chairs are bigger than the old ones.

a. True.					b. False.					c. Not given.

A: ___ **3.** The bookshelf ___ many more books.

a. having					b. have						c. has

A: ___ **4.** Helen ___ read all the books yet.

a. didn't					b. hasn't					c. isn't

A: ___ **5.** Helen is happy because she's sitting ___.

a. next to the window		b. in front of the blackboard	c. with the blue computer

A: ___ **6.** Helen still doesn't have a ___.

a. poster					b. computer					c. clock

A: ___ **7.** There's a computer on sale at the ___.

a. supermarket				b. department store			c. classroom

A: ___ **8.** The ___ Peter has now doesn't have an alarm on it.

a. clock					b. desk						c. computer

Answers on Page 206

Lesson 3 — Colors

màu sắc

Learn the words

1. red — đỏ
2. yellow — vàng
3. green — xanh lá
4. blue — xanh da trời
5. purple — tím
6. orange — cam
7. brown — nâu
8. pink — hồng
9. black — đen
10. white — trắng

Q&A Pattern 1

Do you have a <u>blue</u> pencil?
No, but I have a blue crayon.

Q&A Pattern 2

What did you get for your birthday?
I got this <u>white</u> dress from my aunt.

Q&A Pattern 3

What color are you going to choose?
I'm going to choose <u>purple</u>.

Conversation 1

Cody: The art teacher wants us to make a poster for homework.

Kate: I know. I don't have many colored pencils.

Cody: Me, neither. I need a <u>green</u> pencil for the grass in my picture.

Kate: You can borrow mine. Do you have a <u>blue</u> pencil?

Cody: No, but I have a <u>blue</u> crayon.

Kate: That's fine. What color do you think the car should be?

Cody: I think it should be <u>black</u>.

Kate: The road is <u>black</u>. I think the car should be <u>yellow</u>.

Cody: I hope you have a <u>red</u> pencil for the stop sign.

Kate: I don't have one. I can't finish my poster without a <u>red</u> pencil!

Answer the questions

1. What do they have to make for homework?
2. Why does Cody want a green pencil?
3. What did Cody lend to Kate?
4. Which color does Kate need to finish her poster?

Put the sentences in order

Cody needs a green pencil for the grass in his picture. ___

Kate can't finish her poster because she doesn't have a red pencil. ___

The art teacher wants the students to make a poster. (1)

Kate borrows Cody's blue crayon. ___

Conversation 2

Cody: Happy birthday Kate! What did you get for your birthday?

Kate: I got this <u>white</u> dress from my aunt. Dad is going to get me a new bike.

Cody: That's amazing! What color are you going to choose?

Kate: I'm going to choose <u>purple</u>. Hopefully, the bike shop has one.

Cody: Why do you need a new bike?

Kate: The bike I have now is too small. I've already had it for five years.

Cody: Are you talking about the <u>pink</u> bike?

Kate: Yes, I am. It's the only one I've ever had.

Cody: You definitely need a new one! I also have a gift for you.

Kate: A packet of colored pencils. This is just what I need. Thank you!

Answer the questions

1. What did Kate's aunt give her for her birthday?
2. What color bike is Kate going to choose?
3. How long has Kate had her pink bike?
4. What did Cody give to Kate for her birthday?

Noun, Verb or Adjective?

choose ☐ Noun ☐ Verb ☐ ADJ   **new** ☐ Noun ☐ Verb ☐ ADJ

has ☐ Noun ☐ Verb ☐ ADJ   **bike** ☐ Noun ☐ Verb ☐ ADJ

amazing ☐ Noun ☐ Verb ☐ ADJ   **talking** ☐ Noun ☐ Verb ☐ ADJ

packet ☐ Noun ☐ Verb ☐ ADJ   **small** ☐ Noun ☐ Verb ☐ ADJ

Take the test

Write the answer next to the letter "A"

A: ___ **1.** The ___ teacher wants the students to make a poster.

a. art   b. English   c. math

A: ___ **2.** Kate ___ have many colored pencils.

a. don't   b. isn't   c. doesn't

A: ___ **3.** Cody can lend Kate a ___.

a. blue crayon   b. green pencil   c. blue pencil

A: ___ **4.** Kate needs a ___ pencil to finish her poster.

a. green   b. blue   c. red

A: ___ **5.** Kate's ___ gave her the white dress.

a. dad   b. aunt   c. friend

A: ___ **6.** Kate wants to choose a ___ bike.

a. yellow   b. purple   c. pink

A: ___ **7.** Kate has had her bike ___ five years.

a. of   b. on   c. for

A: ___ **8.** Cody gave Kate a packet ___ colored pencils.

a. of   b. for   c. with

Answers on Page 206

Lesson 4 — My family

gia đình của tôi

Learn the words

1. grandmother
   bà
2. grandfather
   ông
3. baby sister
   em gái
4. baby brother
   em trai
5. aunt
   cô
6. uncle
   chú
7. sister
   chị
8. brother
   anh
9. mother
   mẹ
10. father
    bố

Q&A Pattern 1

Who was that person you were talking to?
That person was my <u>aunt</u>.

Q&A Pattern 2

Do you enjoy spending time with your <u>aunt</u>?
Yes, we have a lot of fun together.

Q&A Pattern 3

What will you be doing this weekend?
I'll be spending time with my <u>grandmother</u>.

Conversation 1

Ben: Who was that person you were talking to?

Jane: That person was my <u>aunt</u>. She is staying at our house for a week.

Ben: She looks very young to be your <u>aunt</u>.

Jane: That's what my <u>sister</u> always says.

Ben: Why is she staying at your house?

Jane: <u>Uncle</u> Frank is going on a camping trip with my <u>father</u>.

Ben: Doesn't your <u>aunt</u> like being at home alone?

Jane: No, she doesn't. So, my mother invited her to stay with us instead.

Ben: Do you enjoy spending time with your <u>aunt</u>?

Jane: Yes, we have a lot of fun together.

Answer the questions

1. How long is Jane's aunt staying at her house?

2. What does Ben think about Jane's aunt?

3. What is Uncle Frank doing with Jane's father?

4. Who invited Jane's aunt to stay with them?

Unscramble the words

1. talking / her / Jane / aunt / was / to

2. looks / young / Jane's / aunt / Ben / thinks

3. on / camping / a / going / Uncle / trip / Frank / is

4. have / together / a / of / Jane / her / lot / aunt / fun / and

Conversation 2

Jane: What will you be doing this weekend?

Ben: I'll be spending time with my <u>grandmother</u>.

Jane: Is she still in hospital?

Ben: No, she's at home now. She's feeling much better.

Jane: Did she like the card you and your <u>brothers</u> made for her?

Ben: Yes, she thought the picture I drew of my <u>grandfather</u> was funny.

Jane: How is your <u>grandfather</u> these days?

Ben: He's very busy. He has to do all the chores around the house.

Jane: Does the doctor want your <u>grandmother</u> to take a rest?

Ben: Yes, the doctor told her to stay in bed for five days.

Answer the questions

1. Where is Ben's grandmother now?

2. What did Ben's grandmother think of his drawing?

3. Why is Ben's grandfather busy?

4. What did the doctor tell Ben's grandmother to do?

Find three nouns, verbs and adjectives

Nouns	Verbs	Adjectives
1. _____	1. _____	2. _____
2. _____	2. _____	2. _____
3. _____	3. _____	3. _____

Take the test

Write the answer next to the letter "A"

A: ___ **1.** Jane was ___ to her aunt.

a. talk   b. talked   c. talking

A: ___ **2.** Jane's aunt is staying at her house for a ___.

a. day   b. week   c. weekend

A: ___ **3.** Jane has a sister.

a. True.   b. False.   c. Not given.

A: ___ **4.** Jane enjoys ___ time with her aunt.

a. to spend   b. have spent   c. spending

A: ___ **5.** Ben's ___ was in hospital.

a. grandmother   b. grandfather   c. uncle

A: ___ **6.** Ben drew a funny picture of his ___.

a. father   b. grandmother   c. grandfather

A: ___ **7.** Ben's grandfather ___ to do all the chores.

a. must   b. has   c. have

A: ___ **8.** The doctor told Ben's grandmother to ___.

a. stay in hospital   b. stay in bed   c. do all the chores

Answers on Page 206

Lesson 5: Shapes

hình dạng

Learn the words

1. square
   hình vuông
2. circle
   hình tròn
3. triangle
   tam giác
4. oval
   hình bầu dục
5. diamond
   hình kim cương
6. star
   ngôi sao
7. rectangle
   hình chữ nhật
8. octagon
   hình bát giác
9. heart
   hình trái tim
10. pentagon
    hình năm cánh

Q&A Pattern 1

What is a stop sign in the shape of?
A stop sign is in the shape of an <u>octagon</u>.

Q&A Pattern 2

Which shape would you like to get?
I think a <u>square</u> coffee table would be better.

Q&A Pattern 3

What other shapes are coffee tables made in?
Coffee tables are also made in the shape of a <u>rectangle</u>.

Conversation 1

Mom: What did you learn about at school today?

Kate: We learned about street signs.

Mom: It's important to know what they all mean.

Kate: There's a test tomorrow. We have to learn them all by <u>heart</u>.

Mom: What is a stop sign in the shape of?

Kate: A stop sign is in the shape of an <u>octagon</u>. That's an easy one.

Mom: Are there any signs in the shape of a <u>triangle</u>?

Kate: Yes, there's one in front of our school for the pedestrian crossing.

Mom: Most street signs that caution people are <u>diamond</u>-shaped.

Kate: That's easy to remember. I think the test won't be too difficult.

Answer the questions

1. What does Kate need to learn by heart?

2. Is a stop sign in the shape of a pentagon?

3. Where is the sign for the pedestrian crossing?

4. What does Kate think about tomorrow's test?

Fill in the blanks

Mom: What _____ you _____ about at _____ today?

Kate: _____ learned _____ street _____.

Mom: It's _____ to _____ what they _____ mean.

Kate: There's a test _____. We _____ to learn _____ all by _____.

Conversation 2

Dad: We need a new coffee table. I think we should buy one today.

Kate: What's wrong with the coffee table we have now?

Dad: It's too small and we've had it for a long time.

Mom: I also don't like the shape of it. Don't buy a table in the shape of a <u>circle</u>.

Kate: Which shape would you like to get?

Mom: I think a <u>square</u> coffee table would be better.

Kate: What other shapes are coffee tables made in?

Dad: Coffee tables are also made in the shape of a <u>rectangle</u>.

Mom: I saw an <u>oval</u>-shaped one a few days ago.

Dad: I'm going to the furniture store now. I'll get a <u>square</u> coffee table.

Answer the questions

1. Why doesn't Mom like the coffee table they have now?
2. Which shape does Mom want the new coffee table to be in?
3. Are there <u>oval</u>-shaped coffee tables?
4. Where is Dad going now?

Past, Present or Future?

1. We need a new coffee table.   ☐ **Past** ☐ **Present** ☐ **Future**

2. Don't buy a table in the shape of a circle.   ☐ **Past** ☐ **Present** ☐ **Future**

3. I saw an oval-shaped one a few days ago.   ☐ **Past** ☐ **Present** ☐ **Future**

4. I'll get a square coffee table.   ☐ **Past** ☐ **Present** ☐ **Future**

Take the test

Write the answer next to the letter "A"

A: ___ 1. The students were learning ___ street signs today.

a. for							b. of							c. about

A: ___ 2. The students have to learn all the street signs ___ heart.

a. to							b. by							c. be

A: ___ 3. A stop sign is ___ the shape of an octagon.

a. on							b. in							c. by

A: ___ 4. Most street signs that caution people are ___ ones.

a. triangle-shaped			b. square-shaped			c. diamond-shaped

A: ___ 5. Dad ___ to buy a new coffee table.

a. want						b. wanting					c. wants

A: ___ 6. The coffee table they have now is too ___.

a. big							b. small						c. ugly

A: ___ 7. Mom would like a ___ coffee table.

a. circle						b. square					c. oval

A: ___ 8. Which shape is a coffee table not made in?

a. An oval.					b. A rectangle.				c. A pentagon.

Answers on Page 206

Lesson 6: At the zoo

ở sở thú

Learn the words

1. monkey
   con khỉ
2. lion
   sư tử
3. tiger
   con hổ
4. bear
   gấu
5. rhino
   tê giác
6. penguin
   chim cánh cụt
7. giraffe
   hươu cao cổ
8. elephant
   con voi
9. crocodile
   cá sấu
10. kangaroo
    kăng-gu-ru (chuột túi)

Q&A Pattern 1

Which animal do you want to see first?
I want to see the <u>bears</u> first.

Q&A Pattern 2

Are there <u>rhinos</u> at this zoo?
No, there aren't.

Q&A Pattern 3

Which animal was your favorite?
My favorite animal was the <u>giraffe</u>.

Conversation 1

Paul: Which animal do you want to see first?

Brad: I want to see the <u>bears</u> first.

Paul: Let's look at the zoo map. The <u>bears</u> are quite far away.

Brad: We can stop and look at other animals on the way.

Paul: The <u>kangaroos</u> are on this road. I want to see them.

Brad: The <u>lions</u> are also nearby. We should look at them, too.

Paul: Are there <u>rhinos</u> at this zoo?

Brad: No, there aren't. There are <u>elephants</u>. One of them is a baby.

Paul: We have to see the baby <u>elephant</u>!

Brad: I agree. We'll go to the <u>elephants</u> last.

Answer the questions

1. Which animal does Brad want to see first?

2. What is Paul looking at?

3. Will the boys be looking at rhinos today?

4. Which animal will they see last?

True or False?

1. Paul wants to see the bears first. ☐ **True** ☐ **False**

2. There is a baby elephant at the zoo. ☐ **True** ☐ **False**

3. The boys don't want to see the kangaroos. ☐ **True** ☐ **False**

4. There aren't any rhinos at the zoo. ☐ **True** ☐ **False**

Conversation 2

Brad: We had the best day at the zoo today.

Paul: I know! We were lucky to see so many animals being fed.

Brad: The penguins were the funniest. They really love to eat fish!

Paul: The monkeys were also funny.

Brad: One of the monkeys didn't like to share the fruit.

Paul: Watching the crocodiles being fed made me nervous.

Brad: The zookeeper is very brave. I wouldn't like to have that job.

Paul: Which animal was your favorite?

Brad: My favorite animal was the giraffe.

Paul: Watching it eat the leaves was interesting.

Answer the questions

1. Why did Brad think they were lucky today?

2. What do penguins love to eat?

3. How did Brad describe the zookeeper?

4. What was the giraffe eating?

Write the adjectives

1. They were _____ to see so many animals at the zoo.

2. Brad thought the penguins were the _____ .

3. Watching the zookeeper feed the crocodiles made Paul _____ .

4. Brad thinks the zookeeper is very _____ .

Take the test

Write the answer next to the letter "A"

A: ___ **1.** Brad wants to see the ___ first.

a. bears　　　　　　　　　　b. lions　　　　　　　　　　c. elephants

A: ___ **2.** "We can stop and look at other animals on the ___."

a. road　　　　　　　　　　b. way　　　　　　　　　　c. zoo map

A: ___ **3.** There are no ___ at the zoo.

a. rhinos　　　　　　　　　　b. kangaroos　　　　　　　　　　c. lions

A: ___ **4.** There is a baby ___ at the zoo.

a. bear　　　　　　　　　　b. elephant　　　　　　　　　　c. lion

A: ___ **5.** Brad thought the penguins were the ___.

a. most fun　　　　　　　　　　b. funniest　　　　　　　　　　c. funnest

A: ___ **6.** One of ___ didn't like to share the fruit.

a. monkey　　　　　　　　　　b. the monkeys　　　　　　　　　　c. the monkey

A: ___ **7.** The crocodiles ate a lot of food.

a. True　　　　　　　　　　b. False　　　　　　　　　　c. Not given

A: ___ **8.** Brad's favorite animal was the ___.

a. kangaroo　　　　　　　　　　b. giraffe　　　　　　　　　　c. elephant

Answers on Page 206

Lesson 7 — Jobs

công việc

Learn the words

1. doctor
   bác sĩ
2. chef
   đầu bếp
3. nurse
   y tá
4. police officer
   cảnh sát
5. taxi driver
   tài xế taxi

6. teacher
   giáo viên
7. farmer
   nông dân
8. salesclerk
   người bán hàng
9. firefighter
   lính cứu hỏa
10. builder
    người xây dựng

Q&A Pattern 1

What does your father do?
My father is a <u>doctor</u>.

Q&A Pattern 2

Do you want to be a <u>chef</u> when you're older?
Yes, I think that would be a good job for me.

Q&A Pattern 3

Do you think I'd make a good <u>farmer</u>?
Yes, I do.

Conversation 1

Candice: My father just called and said he's going to be working late.

Sally: What does your father do?

Candice: My father is a doctor. He works at the hospital.

Sally: Does your mother work at the same one?

Candice: Yes, she does. She's a nurse there.

Sally: Wasn't your mother a salesclerk before?

Candice: Yes, but that was a long time ago. She worked at a shoe shop.

Sally: Was she a student at that time?

Candice: Yes, she was. She didn't like that job, but she needed money.

Sally: My father was a taxi driver when he was studying at university.

Answer the questions

1. Who is going to be working late?
2. Where does Candice's father work?
3. Why did Candice's mother work at a shoe shop?
4. When was Sally's father a taxi driver?

Complete the sentences using three words

1. Candice's father is going to _____ .
2. Candice's father works _____ .
3. Sally's mother worked at _____ .
4. Sally's father was a taxi driver when he was _____ .

Conversation 2

Sally: The <u>teacher</u> wants us to think about what job we'd like to have.

Candice: I don't know what I want to do yet.

Sally: My father wants me to be a <u>police officer</u> like him.

Candice: I don't think that's a good job for you. You're too shy.

Sally: I agree. I'd like to open a small restaurant.

Candice: Do you want to be a <u>chef</u> when you're older?

Sally: Yes, I think that would be a good job for me.

Candice: Do you think I'd make a good <u>farmer</u>?

Sally: Yes, I do. You already know how to grow vegetables.

Candice: Growing a few tomatoes doesn't make me good at farming!

Answer the questions

1. What does Sally's father want her to be?
2. Why does Candice think Sally wouldn't be a good police officer?
3. What does Sally want to do?
4. Why does Sally think Candice would make a good farmer?

Which person?

1. _____ doesn't know what she wants to do yet.
2. _____ would like to open a small restaurant.
3. _____ thinks being a chef would be a good job for her.
4. _____ knows how to grow vegetables.

Take the test

Write the answer next to the letter "A"

A: ___ **1.** Candice's father is a ___.

a. nurse
b. police officer
c. doctor

A: ___ **2.** Candice's mother ___ a salesclerk before.

a. is
b. was
c. will be

A: ___ **3.** Candice's mother works at the ___ now.

a. university
b. shoe shop
c. hospital

A: ___ **4.** Candice's parents work at the same place.

a. True.
b. False.
c. Not given.

A: ___ **5.** Sally's father wants her to be a ___.

a. firefighter
b. doctor
c. police officer

A: ___ **6.** Sally would like to be a ___ when she is older.

a. nurse
b. chef
c. farmer

A: ___ **7.** Sally ___ Candice would make a good farmer.

a. doesn't think
b. thinks
c. isn't sure if

A: ___ **8.** Which job was not mentioned?

a. A teacher.
b. A taxi driver.
c. A builder.

Answers on Page 206

Lesson 8: At the fruit shop

tại chợ trái cây

Learn the words

1. **apple** — táo
2. **orange** — trái cam
3. **lemon** — Chanh
4. **banana** — trái chuối
5. **watermelon** — dưa hấu
6. **pineapple** — dứa
7. **strawberry** — dâu
8. **grape** — nho
9. **cherry** — quả anh đào
10. **pear** — Lê

Q&A Pattern 1

Which fruit do you want to put in the smoothie?
I want to put <u>banana</u> and <u>strawberry</u> in the smoothie.

Q&A Pattern 2

Are <u>pineapples</u> in season right now?
Yes, I saw some <u>pineapples</u> at the supermarket.

Q&A Pattern 3

Can I eat a <u>pear</u> now?
Yes, you can.

Conversation 1

Dad: Joe wants to make everyone a fruit smoothie.

Helen: Don't put any lemon in mine. It's too sour.

Joe: Don't worry. This one is going to be delicious.

Dad: Which fruit do you want to put in the smoothie?

Joe: I want to put banana and strawberry in the smoothie.

Dad: We also have some apples.

Joe: No, Mom wants to use them to make an apple pie.

Helen: There are also some oranges in the fruit bowl.

Joe: Oranges won't taste good in this smoothie.

Dad: They're good to eat. I'd like to have one right now.

Answer the questions

1. Why doesn't Helen want lemon in her smoothie?

2. What does Mom want to make?

3. Where are the oranges?

4. Which fruit does Dad want to eat?

Noun, Verb or Adjective?

smoothie ☐ Noun ☐ Verb ☐ ADJ

delicious ☐ Noun ☐ Verb ☐ ADJ

worry ☐ Noun ☐ Verb ☐ ADJ

strawberry ☐ Noun ☐ Verb ☐ ADJ

good ☐ Noun ☐ Verb ☐ ADJ

fruit ☐ Noun ☐ Verb ☐ ADJ

sour ☐ Noun ☐ Verb ☐ ADJ

put ☐ Noun ☐ Verb ☐ ADJ

Conversation 2

Mom: Look at the size of this watermelon. It's huge!

Helen: Where did you buy it?

Mom: I bought it at the night market.

Joe: It's the biggest one I've ever seen.

Dad: Are pineapples in season right now?

Mom: Yes, I saw some pineapples at the supermarket.

Dad: You should have gotten one.

Mom: I'll get one next time I go shopping. However, I did get some pears.

Joe: Can I eat a pear now?

Mom: Yes, you can. We can eat the watermelon after dinner.

Answer the questions

1. Which two fruits did Mom buy at the supermarket?

2. Are pineapples in season?

3. What does Joe want to eat now?

4. When will they eat the watermelon?

Put the sentences in order

Mom saw some pineapples at the supermarket. ___

Joe wants to eat a pear now. ___

Mom thinks the watermelon is huge. (1)

It's the biggest watermelon Joe has ever seen. ___

Take the test

Write the answer next to the letter "A"

A: ___ **1.** Helen doesn't want ___ in her smoothie.

a. orange   b. lemon   c. pineapple

A: ___ **2.** Joe put ___ and ___ in the smoothie.

a. lemons, oranges   b. apples, cherry   c. bananas, strawberries

A: ___ **3.** Mom needs ___ for the pie she wants to make.

a. apples   b. pineapples   c. strawberries

A: ___ **4.** "___ are also some oranges in the fruit bowl."

a. They're   b. They   c. There

A: ___ **5.** Mom thinks the ___ is huge.

a. pineapple   b. watermelon   c. pear

A: ___ **6.** Mom bought the watermelon at the ___.

a. fruit market   b. night market   c. supermarket

A: ___ **7.** Joe ___ to eat a pear now.

a. wants   b. want   c. doesn't want

A: ___ **8.** Pineapples are ___ season right now.

a. in   b. on   c. at

Answers on Page 206

Lesson 9: The body

cơ thể

Learn the words

1. **arm** — cánh tay
2. **stomach** — bụng
3. **shoulder** — vai
4. **head** — đầu
5. **neck** — cổ
6. **toe** — ngón chân
7. **foot** — bàn chân
8. **finger** — ngón tay
9. **hand** — bàn tay
10. **leg** — chân

Q&A Pattern 1

What happened to your <u>arm</u>?
I hurt my <u>arm</u> playing soccer.

Q&A Pattern 2

Can you move your <u>hands</u>?
Yes, I can move my <u>hands</u>.

Q&A Pattern 3

How do you feel now?
My <u>stomach</u> feels a little sore.

Conversation 1

Brad: Hey Stan, do you want to play tennis with me today?

Stan: I can't today. It would be difficult for me to hit a ball.

Brad: What happened to your <u>arm</u>?

Stan: I hurt my <u>arm</u> playing soccer.

Brad: Did you get pushed over during the game?

Stan: No, I tried to <u>head</u> the ball and fell on my <u>shoulder</u>.

Brad: We can play something else.

Stan: Sure, but something where I don't need to move my body.

Brad: My brother has a new video game. Can you move your <u>hands</u>?

Stan: Yes, I can move my <u>hands</u>. Let's play!

Answer the questions

1. Which sport does Stan want to play?

2. Why is it difficult for Stan to hit a ball?

3. How did Stan hurt his arm?

4. What are they going to play?

Unscramble the words

1. for / be / a / ball / It / Stan / to / hit / would / difficult

2. arm / soccer / playing / Stan / his / hurt

3. Stan / fell / on / his / shoulder

4. video / new / game / a / brother / Brad's / has

Conversation 2

Stan: How was swim practice today?

Brad: Not bad. The coach said I need to kick my <u>legs</u> more.

Stan: It's important to keep your <u>feet</u> moving.

Brad: I also swam a little faster when I kept my <u>fingers</u> together.

Stan: How many laps did you swim today?

Brad: I swam twenty laps of the pool.

Stan: That's pretty good. How do you feel now?

Brad: My <u>stomach</u> feels a little sore.

Stan: I think you need to exercise more.

Brad: That's what the coach said as well!

Answer the questions

1. What does the coach want Brad to do?

2. How many laps of the pool did Brad swim?

3. How is Brad's stomach feeling?

4. What does Stan think Brad needs to do?

Find three nouns, verbs and adjectives

Nouns　　　　　**Verbs**　　　　　**Adjectives**

1. _____　　1. _____　　2. _____

2. _____　　2. _____　　2. _____

3. _____　　3. _____　　3. _____

Take the test

Write the answer next to the letter "A"

A: ___ **1.** Brad wanted to play ___ with Stan at first.

a. soccer   ب. tennis   c. video games

A: ___ **2.** Stan fell on his ___.

a. hand   b. shoulder   c. head

A: ___ **3.** Stan hurt his arm playing ___.

a. tennis   b. volleyball   c. soccer

A: ___ **4.** They decided to play a video game because Stan can move his ___.

a. shoulders   b. hands   c. arms

A: ___ **5.** Brad needs to kick ___ legs more when he is swimming.

a. he's   b. him   c. his

A: ___ **6.** "I also swam a little faster when I kept my ___ together."

a. fingers   b. legs   c. feet

A: ___ **7.** Brad swam ___ laps of the pool.

a. forty   b. thirty   c. twenty

A: ___ **8.** Stan thinks Brad should ___ more.

a. swim   b. exercise   c. kick his legs

Answers on Page 206

Lesson 10: Sports

thể thao

Learn the words

1. **basketball** — bóng rổ
2. **badminton** — cầu lông
3. **golf** — gôn
4. **hockey** — khúc côn cầu
5. **soccer** — bóng đá
6. **cricket** — bóng gậy (bóng Crích-kê)
7. **baseball** — bóng chày
8. **volleyball** — bóng chuyền
9. **football** — bóng đá
10. **tennis** — quần vợt

Q&A Pattern 1

Which sport would you like to learn how to play?
I would like to learn how to play <u>badminton</u>.

Q&A Pattern 2

When do you want to play <u>badminton</u>?
I can play <u>badminton</u> this afternoon.

Q&A Pattern 3

How was the <u>baseball</u> game?
It was great because my team won!

Conversation 1

Helen: I want to learn a new sport.

Jane: Which sport would you like to learn how to play?

Helen: I would like to learn how to play badminton.

Jane: That sounds like fun. I would like to learn, too.

Helen: We both already play tennis. It shouldn't be too difficult.

Jane: Should we find a coach to teach us badminton?

Helen: I think we should try for fun first.

Jane: Good idea. I tried to play golf, but didn't enjoy it.

Helen: Great! When do you want to play badminton?

Jane: I can play badminton this afternoon. I'm watching a baseball game now.

Answer the questions

1. Which sport does Helen want to learn how to play?
2. Do they want to find a coach to teach them first?
3. When will they play badminton?
4. What is Jane watching now?

Fill in the blanks

Jane: Which _____ would you _____ to learn _____ to play?

Helen: I _____ like to _____ how to play _____.

Jane: That _____ like _____. I would _____ _____ learn, too.

Helen: We both _____ play _____. It _____ be too _____.

Conversation 2

Helen: Thanks for meeting me today.

Jane: I'm excited to learn how to play <u>badminton</u>.

Helen: How was the <u>baseball</u> game?

Jane: It was great because my team won!

Helen: My <u>basketball</u> team wasn't so lucky. They lost by one point.

Jane: That's too bad. I'll be watching a <u>cricket</u> match this evening.

Helen: I don't know anything about that sport.

Jane: Neither do I. A friend from England wants to watch it with me.

Helen: It looks like you'll be learning about two sports today.

Jane: I love all sports, except for <u>golf</u>. Let's get started!

Answer the questions

1. Whose sports team won?

2. How much did Helen's basketball team lose by?

3. Where does Jane have a friend from?

4. Which sport does Jane not like?

Past, Present or Future?

1. I'm excited to learn how to play badminton.   ☐ **Past** ☐ **Present** ☐ **Future**

2. My basketball team wasn't so lucky.   ☐ **Past** ☐ **Present** ☐ **Future**

3. I'll be watching a cricket match this evening.   ☐ **Past** ☐ **Present** ☐ **Future**

4. I don't know anything about that sport.   ☐ **Past** ☐ **Present** ☐ **Future**

Take the test

Write the answer next to the letter "A"

A: ___ **1.** Helen wants ___ a new sport.

a. learning   b. learn   c. to learn

A: ___ **2.** Helen would like to learn how to play ___.

a. badminton   b. tennis   c. golf

A: ___ **3.** Jane and Helen both play ___.

a. baseball   b. badminton   c. tennis

A: ___ **4.** Jane is watching baseball with her father.

a. True   b. False   c. Not given

A: ___ **5.** Jane's baseball team ___.

a. won   b. didn't win   c. hadn't won

A: ___ **6.** Helen doesn't know ___ about cricket.

a. anything   b. something   c. everything

A: ___ **7.** "I love all sports, except ___ golf."

a. to   b. for   c. to

A: ___ **8.** Which sport was not mentioned?

a. Cricket.   b. Basketball.   c. Volleyball.

Answers on Page 206

Lesson 11: Places

nơi chốn

Learn the words

1. store
   cửa hàng
2. swimming pool
   hồ bơi
3. department store
   cửa hàng bách hóa
4. supermarket
   siêu thị
5. night market
   chợ đêm
6. cinema
   rạp chiếu phim
7. beach
   bãi biển
8. park
   công viên
9. gym
   phòng thể dục
10. restaurant
    nhà hàng

Q&A Pattern 1

What's the best thing about living in this town?
The best thing about living here is the <u>beach</u>.

Q&A Pattern 2

Is there a <u>cinema</u> nearby?
Yes, there is one.

Q&A Pattern 3

Do you know any good <u>restaurants</u> in the city?
Yes, I know the best <u>restaurants</u>.

Conversation 1

Chris: What's the best thing about living in this town?

Brody: The best thing about living here is the <u>beach</u>.

Chris: The <u>beach</u> is nice, but your town isn't very good for shopping.

Brody: That's true. It's definitely not like the city.

Chris: I like the city because you can buy anything you want.

Brody: There's no <u>department store</u>, but we do have a big <u>supermarket</u>.

Chris: What do you do if you can't find something you need?

Brody: I usually order what I need from an online <u>store</u>.

Chris: Do you think you'll ever move to the city one day?

Brody: No, I love it here too much!

Answer the questions

1. What does Brody like about living in her town?
2. Why wouldn't Chris like living in the town?
3. Does Brody's town have a department store?
4. Does Brody want to move to the city?

True or False?

1. Brody likes living near the beach.   ☐ **True** ☐ **False**
2. Chris likes the city because it's easier to buy things.   ☐ **True** ☐ **False**
3. There is a department store in Brody's town.   ☐ **True** ☐ **False**
4. Brody is thinking about moving to the city.   ☐ **True** ☐ **False**

Conversation 2

Brody: I'm thinking about going to the city next Saturday.

Chris: Great! I can meet you at the train station.

Brody: I'm actually going to take the bus there.

Chris: I'll wait for you at the bus stop. There's a great <u>park</u> across from there.

Brody: I'd like to see a movie. Is there a cinema nearby?

Chris: Yes, there is one. We can go there after lunch.

Brody: Do you know any good <u>restaurants</u> in the city?

Chris: Yes, I know the best <u>restaurants</u>.

Brody: Ok, great. After the movie, we can visit a <u>night market</u>.

Chris: That's a great idea. I'll see you next week.

Answer the questions

1. How will Brody go to the city?

2. Where is the park?

3. Does Chris know any good restaurants in the city?

4. Where will they go after the movie?

Write the nouns

1. Brody is thinking about going to the _____ next Saturday.

2. They are going to see a _____ after lunch.

3. Chris knows the best _____ in the city.

4. Brody wants to go to the night _____ after the movie.

Take the test

Write the answer next to the letter "A"

A: ___ 1. "The ___ thing about living here is the beach."

a. most   b. favorite   c. best

A: ___ 2. Chris thinks Brody's town isn't good ___ shopping.

a. to   b. for   c. at

A: ___ 3. Brody's town has a big ___.

a. department store   b. supermarket   c. online store

A: ___ 4. Brody ___ she'll every move to the city.

a. won't think   b. don't think   c. doesn't think

A: ___ 5. They will meet at the ___.

a. train station   b. bus stop   c. cinema

A: ___ 6. They will go to the ___ after lunch.

a. cinema   b. restaurant   c. night market

A: ___ 7. Chris doesn't know any good restaurants.

a. True.   b. False.   c. Not given.

A: ___ 8. Which place was not mentioned?

a. Gym.   b. Park.   c. Beach.

Answers on Page 206

Lesson 12: Clothes

quần áo

Learn the words

1. **T-shirt** — áo thun
2. **blouse** — sơ mi trắng
3. **dress** — trang phục
4. **coat** — áo khoác
5. **scarf** — khăn quàng cổ
6. **hat** — nón
7. **sweater** — áo len
8. **necktie** — cà vạt
9. **skirt** — váy
10. **jacket** — áo khoác

Q&A Pattern 1

What are you going to wear to the party?
I'm going to wear this blue <u>dress</u>.

Q&A Pattern 2

Do you think I should wear a <u>sweater</u>?
No, I think you should wear a <u>blouse</u>.

Q&A Pattern 3

Won't it be too cold for a <u>T-shirt</u>?
Yes, it will be.

Conversation 1

Fran: What are you going to wear to the party?

Pam: I'm going to wear this blue <u>dress</u>.

Fran: That's beautiful. Where did you get it?

Pam: My father got it for me a year ago. I have never worn it.

Fran: It looks like the weather is going to be quite cold.

Pam: That's okay. I have this <u>jacket</u> I can bring.

Fran: I'm going to bring my <u>coat</u> that you gave me for my birthday.

Pam: Great! That's a warm one.

Fran: I still don't know what to wear. I need some new clothes.

Pam: Let's go shopping together. It'll be fun!

Answer the questions

1. What color is Pam's dress?
2. When did Pam's father get her a dress?
3. What's the weather going to be like?
4. Why did Pam give Fran a coat?

Complete the sentences using three words

1. Pam is going to wear _____.
2. Pam's father gave her the dress _____.
3. Fran still doesn't know _____.
4. Pam thinks it will be fun to _____.

Conversation 2

Fran: Thank you for going shopping with me.

Pam: It's no problem. I love shopping for clothes!

Fran: Do you think I should wear a <u>sweater</u>?

Pam: No, I think you should wear this <u>blouse</u>.

Fran: I don't like it. It's too fancy.

Pam: How about this <u>T-Shirt</u>? You could wear it to the party.

Fran: Won't it be too cold for a <u>T-shirt</u>?

Pam: Yes, it will be. If you get too cold, you can wear your <u>coat</u>.

Fran: It is a very nice <u>T-shirt</u>. Let me try it on.

Pam: While you're trying it on, I'm going to buy this black <u>hat</u>.

Answer the questions

1. Who loves shopping for clothes?
2. Why doesn't Fran like the blouse?
3. What does Fran think of the T-shirt?
4. What is Pam going to buy?

Which person?

1. _____ doesn't like the blouse.
2. _____ doesn't think Fran should wear a sweater.
3. _____ suggests to wear a coat if it gets too cold.
4. _____ wants to try the T-shirt on.

Take the test

Write the answer next to the letter "A"

A: ___ **1.** Pam is going to wear a blue ___ to the party.

a. blouse   b. dress   c. skirt

A: ___ **2.** Pam has never ___ her father's gift.

a. wear   b. wore   c. worn

A: ___ **3.** Pam gave Fran a ___ for her birthday.

a. jacket   b. coat   c. dress

A: ___ **4.** Fran needs ___ some new clothes.

a. to buy   b. buy   c. buying

A: ___ **5.** Pam loves shopping ___ clothes.

a. about   b. of   c. for

A: ___ **6.** Fran thinks the blouse is too ___.

a. fancy   b. cold   c. nice

A: ___ **7.** Fran will wear a ___ to the party.

a. blouse   b. T-shirt   c. sweater

A: ___ **8.** Pam is going to buy a ___ hat.

a. white   b. blue   c. black

Answers on Page 206

Lesson 13: School subjects

những môn học ở trường

Learn the words

1. **English**
   Anh văn
2. **computer class**
   tin học
3. **social studies**
   các môn xã hội
4. **geography**
   Địa lí
5. **physical education (P.E.)**
   Thể dục
6. **art**
   Mỹ thuật
7. **math**
   Toán
8. **science**
   khoa học
9. **history**
   Lịch sử
10. **music**
    Âm Nhạc

Q&A Pattern 1

Why didn't you do well in <u>science</u> this year?
<u>Science</u> was difficult this year.

Q&A Pattern 2

Have you met the new <u>music</u> teacher?
Yes, I have.

Q&A Pattern 3

What's your favorite subject?
My favorite subject is <u>art</u>.

Conversation 1

Mom: I'm happy to see that your grades have improved.

Stan: Me, too. Getting a high grade in history was a surprise.

Mom: Why did you improve so much in this subject?

Stan: I think it's because history was a lot more interesting this year.

Dad: You also did very well in English.

Mom: Stan has always done well in this subject. He needs help with math.

Stan: My friend, Abby, said she can help me with math.

Dad: Why didn't you do well in science this year?

Stan: Science was difficult this year. I don't think I studied hard enough.

Mom: Stan did well in his other subjects, so he should be proud of himself.

Answer the questions

1. Why does Stan think he improved in history?

2. Which subject does Stan always do well in?

3. Who can help Stan with math?

4. Why didn't Stan do well in science this year?

Put the sentences in order

Stan needs help with math. ___

Science was difficult for Stan this year. ___

Mom is happy that Stan's grades have improved. (1)

Stan is surprised that he got a good grade in history. ___

Conversation 2

Stan: I hope I do better in <u>math</u> this year.

Abby: Don't worry. I will help you.

Stan: Thank you. Have you met the new <u>music</u> teacher?

Abby: Yes, I have. She's really friendly.

Stan: I'm excited about <u>computer</u> class this year.

Abby: I find this class a little boring. I hope it gets better.

Stan: What's your favorite subject?

Abby: My favorite subject is <u>art</u>. It's always interesting.

Stan: I'm not good at drawing, so it's difficult for me.

Abby: You are good at <u>P.E.</u>, so perhaps you can help me with this subject.

Answer the questions

1. What does Abby think about the new music teacher?
2. Which subject is Stan excited about?
3. Why does Abby like art?
4. Which subject does Abby need help with?

Noun, Verb or Adjective?

subject ☐ Noun ☐ Verb ☐ ADJ

interesting ☐ Noun ☐ Verb ☐ ADJ

help ☐ Noun ☐ Verb ☐ ADJ

excited ☐ Noun ☐ Verb ☐ ADJ

year ☐ Noun ☐ Verb ☐ ADJ

find ☐ Noun ☐ Verb ☐ ADJ

difficult ☐ Noun ☐ Verb ☐ ADJ

met ☐ Noun ☐ Verb ☐ ADJ

Take the test

Write the answer next to the letter "A"

A: ___ **1.** Mom is happy to see Stan's grades ___ improved.

a. have b. has c. having

A: ___ **2.** ___ a high grade in history was a surprise.

a. Get b. Getting c. Gotten

A: ___ **3.** Stan thinks ___ was a lot more interesting this year.

a. English b. geography c. history

A: ___ **4.** Abby will help Stan with ___.

a. math b. history c. science

A: ___ **5.** Stan hasn't met the new music teacher yet.

a. True. b. False. c. Not given.

A: ___ **6.** Stan is excited about ___ class this year.

a. P.E. b. music c. computer

A: ___ **7.** "I ___ this class a little boring."

a. think b. find c. make

A: ___ **8.** Which school subject was not mentioned?

a. Social studies. b. Art. c. Science.

Answers on Page 206

Lesson 14: Vegetables

rau

Learn the words

1. **potato**
   khoai tây
2. **carrot**
   cà rốt
3. **pumpkin**
   quả bí ngô
4. **broccoli**
   bông cải xanh
5. **asparagus**
   măng tây
6. **cabbage**
   cải bắp
7. **spinach**
   rau bina
8. **corn**
   ngô
9. **onion**
   củ hành
10. **mushroom**
    nấm

Q&A Pattern 1

Which new vegetables do you have in the garden?
I have new pumpkin plants.

Q&A Pattern 2

Can you help me cut up the potatoes?
Yes, I can.

Q&A Pattern 3

Are we going to eat broccoli for dinner?
No, we aren't.

Conversation 1

Ted: Your vegetable garden gets bigger every time I visit.

Grandpa: I like to add new vegetables every year.

Grandma: It's starting to take over the whole backyard!

Ted: Which new vegetables do you have in the garden?

Grandpa: I have new <u>pumpkin</u> plants. And over here is my first <u>carrot</u>.

Grandma: This area is for <u>mushrooms</u>. We'll be eating them for dinner.

Ted: That's amazing! I remember a few years ago, you only had <u>onions</u>.

Grandpa: We also had <u>asparagus</u>, but they didn't grow well.

Grandma: I'd like some of those <u>onions</u> for tonight's dinner.

Grandpa: Ted, go and pick out three big ones for Grandma.

Answer the questions

1. Why is Grandpa's vegetable garden getting bigger?
2. Which new plant has Grandpa added to his vegetable garden?
3. What will they be eating for dinner?
4. How many onions does Grandpa want Ted to get?

Unscramble the words

1. every / vegetables / year / adds / Grandpa / new
2. new / plants / Grandpa / pumpkin / has
3. be / They'll / for / dinner / eating / mushroom
4. grow / didn't / asparagus / The / well

Conversation 2

Ted: Let me help you prepare dinner.

Grandma: Can you help me cut up the <u>potatoes</u>?

Ted: Yes, I can. How do you want them cut?

Grandma: We can make french fries. Cut them into long slices.

Ted: Are we going to eat <u>broccoli</u> for dinner?

Grandma: No, we aren't. There wasn't any at the supermarket.

Ted: What do you cook the <u>mushroom</u> with?

Grandma: I'm going to mix it in with the <u>cabbage</u>.

Ted: That's exactly what Mom does.

Grandma: Of course, she does. I taught her how to cook!

Answer the questions

1. How does Grandma want Ted to cut the potatoes?

2. Was there any broccoli at the supermarket?

3. What is Grandma going to cook the mushroom with?

4. Who taught Ted's mother how to cook cabbage?

Find three nouns, verbs and adjectives

Nouns

1. _____
2. _____
3. _____

Verbs

1. _____
2. _____
3. _____

Adjectives

2. _____
2. _____
3. _____

Take the test

Write the answer next to the letter "A"

A: ___ **1.** The vegetable garden gets bigger ___ time Ted visits.

a. many   b. every   c. any

A: ___ **2.** "It's starting to take ___ the whole backyard!"

a. more   b. on   c. over

A: ___ **3.** Grandpa planted new ___ plants.

a. carrot   b. pumpkin   c. mushroom

A: ___ **4.** Asparagus didn't grow well in Grandpa's garden.

a. True.   b. False.   c. Not given.

A: ___ **5.** ___ is going to cut up the potatoes.

a. Grandma   b. Grandpa   c. Ted

A: ___ **6.** There wasn't any ___ at the supermarket.

a. mushroom   b. broccoli   c. cabbage

A: ___ **7.** Grandma is going to mix the mushroom and ___ together.

a. cabbage   b. potato   c. pumpkin

A: ___ **8.** Grandma ___ Ted's mother how to cook.

a. teached   b. taught   c. teach

Answers on Page 206

Lesson 15: At the toy shop

tại cửa hàng đồ chơi

Learn the words

1. car
   xe hơi
2. airplane
   máy bay
3. dinosaur
   khủng long
4. doll
   búp bê
5. teddy bear
   gấu bông
6. jump rope
   dây nhảy
7. board game
   trò chơi trên bàn cờ
8. toy block
   khối
9. robot
   rô bốt
10. ball
    bóng

Q&A Pattern 1

Whose <u>toy blocks</u> are these?
Those are my baby brother's <u>toy blocks</u>.

Q&A Pattern 2

Do you know where my <u>airplane</u> is?
I think it's in the <u>car</u>.

Q&A Pattern 3

Why don't you play with your new <u>dinosaur</u>?
I've already played with it today.

Conversation 1

Andy: You have so many toys in your bedroom!

Jason: Not all of them are mine. This <u>jump rope</u> belongs to my sister.

Andy: Whose <u>toy blocks</u> are these?

Jason: Those are my baby brother's <u>toy blocks</u>.

Andy: I like this <u>robot</u>. Is it yours?

Jason: Yes, it is. My uncle got it for me.

Andy: Can it do anything interesting?

Jason: Yes, it can walk. It also kicks a <u>ball</u>.

Andy: That's cool! Let's play with it.

Jason: Sorry, we can't. The batteries are flat.

Answer the questions

1. Who does the jump rope belong to?

2. Who gave Jason the robot?

3. What can the robot do?

4. Why can't they play with the robot?

Fill in the blanks

Andy: I _____ this _____. Is it _____?

Jason: Yes, _____ is. My _____ got it _____ me.

Andy: _____ it _____ anything _____?

Jason: Yes, it can _____. It _____ kicks a _____.

Conversation 2

Andy: Do you know where my airplane is?

Mom: I think it's in the car.

Andy: I want to go outside and get it. Where are the keys?

Mom: I'm sorry. Dad drove to the supermarket. He'll be back later.

Andy: Oh, no. I really wanted to play with the airplane.

Mom: Why don't you play with your new dinosaur?

Andy: I've already played with it today.

Mom: Would you like to do something with me?

Andy: I would love to. What can we do?

Mom: Let's play a board game together.

Answer the questions

1. What did Andy want to play with?

2. Where is Andy's airplane?

3. What has Andy already played with today?

4. What are they going to play?

Past, Present or Future?

1. Dad drove to the supermarket.   ☐ **Past** ☐ **Present** ☐ **Future**

2. He'll be back later.   ☐ **Past** ☐ **Present** ☐ **Future**

3. I really wanted to play with the airplane.   ☐ **Past** ☐ **Present** ☐ **Future**

4. Let's play a board game together.   ☐ **Past** ☐ **Present** ☐ **Future**

Take the test

Write the answer next to the letter "A"

A: ___ 1. The jump rope belongs to ___.

a. Jason   b. Jason's sister   c. Andy

A: ___ 2. Andy ___ the robot.

a. like   b. liking   c. likes

A: ___ 3. Jason's ___ got him a robot.

a. uncle   b. sister   c. aunt

A: ___ 4. The robot has four batteries, but they are flat right now.

a. True.   b. False.   c. Not given.

A: ___ 5. Where is Andy's airplane?

a. Outside.   b. In the car.   c. At the supermarket.

A: ___ 6. "I'm sorry, but Dad ___ to the supermarket."

a. drove   b. drives   c. drove

A: ___ 7. Andy has already played with the ___ today.

a. airplane   b. dinosaur   c. board game

A: ___ 8. Who will Andy play the board game with?

a. His father.   b. His mother.   c. Jason.

Answers on Page 206

Lesson 16: In the kitchen

trong bếp

Learn the words

1. **refrigerator**
   tủ lạnh
2. **cupboard**
   cái tủ
3. **microwave oven**
   lò vi song
4. **dish rack**
   giá để đĩa
5. **coffee maker**
   máy pha cà phê
6. **toaster**
   lò nướng bánh mỳ
7. **stove**
   bếp
8. **pan**
   chảo
9. **rice cooker**
   nồi cơm điện
10. **blender**
    máy xay

Q&A Pattern 1

Do you think I should get a <u>microwave oven</u>?
Yes, <u>microwave ovens</u> are very convenient.

Q&A Pattern 2

Have you used the <u>blender</u> yet?
Yes, I have.

Q&A Pattern 3

Where are the plates?
They're in the <u>cupboard</u> on the left.

Conversation 1

Fran: Hi, Pam. How's your new house?

Pam: It's almost ready. I still need to buy some things for the kitchen.

Fran: I have a rice cooker I don't use anymore. Do you want it?

Pam: No, thank you. I already have one. What I need is a blender.

Fran: Let me buy one for you. I want to get you a gift.

Pam: That's very kind of you. Do you think I should get a microwave oven?

Fran: Yes, microwave ovens are very convenient.

Pam: I also need to buy a toaster. I'm using the stove to make toast now.

Fran: That's not very good. We should go shopping today.

Pam: Great! I'll meet you at the department store.

Answer the questions

1. Does Pam want Fran's rice cooker?
2. What does Fran want to get for Pam?
3. What does Fran think about microwave ovens?
4. Where will Pam be meeting Fran?

True or False?

1. Pam doesn't need anything else for the kitchen.   ☐ **True** ☐ **False**

2. Fran often uses her rice cooker.   ☐ **True** ☐ **False**

3. Fran thinks microwave ovens are convenient.   ☐ **True** ☐ **False**

4. The two girls will meet at the department store.   ☐ **True** ☐ **False**

Conversation 2

Pam: Come in and sit down. I'm still cooking dinner.

Fran: That's okay. Have you used the new <u>blender</u> yet?

Pam: Yes, I have. I made some salad dressing with it yesterday.

Fran: Let me help you set the table. Where are the plates?

Pam: They're in the <u>cupboard</u> on the left.

Fran: I see you have a new <u>refrigerator</u>.

Pam: The one I had before was much too small. This one is perfect.

Fran: It looks like you have everything you need for your new kitchen.

Pam: No, I still need a good <u>coffee machine</u>. I'll be getting one soon.

Fran: That's a great idea. Maybe I should get one, too.

Answer the questions

1. What did Pam make with the new blender?

2. Where are the plates?

3. Why did Pam get a new refrigerator?

4. What does Pam still need to get?

Write the verbs

1. Pam was still _____ dinner when Fran arrived.

2. Fran helped _____ the table.

3. The refrigerator Pam _____ before was too small.

4. Pam will be _____ a coffee machine soon.

Take the test

Write the answer next to the letter "A"

A: ____ **1.** Pam ____ needs to buy some things for the kitchen.

a. still   b. already   c. yet

A: ____ **2.** Fran ____ use her rice cooker anymore.

a. don't   b. doesn't   c. hasn't

A: ____ **3.** Fran will buy a ____ for Pam.

a. pan   b. toaster   c. blender

A: ____ **4.** Where is Pam making toast now?

a. In the toaster.   b. On the stove.   c. In the microwave oven.

A: ____ **5.** The ____ are in the cupboard on the left.

a. plates   b. pans   c. dish racks

A: ____ **6.** Pam's old refrigerator was too ____.

a. big   b. small   c. perfect

A: ____ **7.** Pam has everything she needs for her kitchen now.

a. True.   b. False.   c. Not given.

A: ____ **8.** Which kitchen item was not mentioned?

a. Microwave oven.   b. Coffee machine.   c. Pan.

Answers on Page 206

Lesson 17: Feelings

cảm xúc

Learn the words

1. fine — khỏe
2. sad — buồn
3. bored — chán
4. energetic — năng động
5. tired — mệt mỏi
6. angry — giận
7. happy — vui mừng
8. excited — phấn khởi
9. frustrated — bực bội
10. sick — đau ốm

Q&A Pattern 1

How are you feeling?
I'm feeling <u>energetic</u>.

Q&A Pattern 2

Is there something wrong?
I'm a little <u>frustrated</u>.

Q&A Pattern 3

Were your parents <u>angry</u> with you?
No, not at all.

Conversation 1

Abby: It's the first day of the new school year. How are you feeling?

Stan: I'm feeling <u>energetic</u>. I want to get better grades this year.

Abby: We have computer class first, which is not my favorite subject.

Stan: I like learning about computers. Why don't you like it?

Abby: I get a little <u>bored</u> sometimes. The class is too quiet for me.

Stan: Maybe the class will be different this time.

Abby: I'll be <u>fine</u>. At least it only goes for one hour.

Stan: I'm <u>excited</u> about it. I always learn something new.

Abby: That's true. The teacher teaches us a lot.

Stan: That's right! You should be <u>happy</u> about that.

Answer the questions

1. How is Stan feeling about the first day of the new school year?

2. Why doesn't Abby like computer class?

3. How long does computer class go for?

4. What does Stan think Abby should be happy about?

Complete the sentences using three words

1. It's the first day of the _____.

2. This year, Stan wants to _____.

3. Stan likes _____.

4. The computer class only goes _____.

Conversation 2

Stan: Abby, you don't look <u>happy</u>. Is there something wrong?

Abby: I'm a little <u>frustrated</u>. I didn't do well on my math test yesterday.

Stan: That's strange. You're really good at math.

Abby: I studied hard, but still got four questions incorrect.

Stan: I thought the test was quite easy.

Abby: I agree. I don't know why I wrote the wrong answers.

Stan: Maybe you were too <u>tired</u> during the test.

Abby: I was feeling a little <u>sick</u> yesterday. Perhaps that is the reason.

Stan: Were your parents <u>angry</u> with you?

Abby: No, not at all. They knew I was <u>sad</u> about the test result.

Answer the questions

1. Why did Stan think it was strange that Abby did badly on the math test?

2. How many questions did Abby get wrong?

3. How was Abby feeling yesterday?

4. Why weren't Abby's parents angry with her?

Which person?

1. _____ thinks Abby doesn't look happy today.

2. _____ didn't do well on the math test.

3. _____ thought the test was quite easy.

4. _____ studied hard for the math test.

Take the test

Write the answer next to the letter "A"

A: ___ **1.** Stan wants to ___ better grades this year.

a. get   b. gotten   c. getting

A: ___ **2.** Abby gets ___ in computer class.

a. excited   b. bored   c. frustrated

A: ___ **3.** Stan likes learning ___ computers.

a. about   b. around   c. abound

A: ___ **4.** "That's right! You should ___ happy about that."

a. by   b. be   c. been

A: ___ **5.** Abby didn't do ___ on the math test.

a. good   b. goodly   c. well

A: ___ **6.** Abby studied hard, ___ she still got four questions incorrect.

a. because   b. so   c. but

A: ___ **7.** Abby was feeling ___ the day before the test.

a. tired   b. sick   c. frustrated

A: ___ **8.** Abby's parents knew she was feeling ___ about the test result.

a. sad   b. angry   c. sick

Answers on Page 206

Lesson 18: At the ice cream shop

tại cửa hàng kem

Learn the words

1. **mint** — bạc hà
2. **cherry** — quả anh đào
3. **strawberry** — dâu
4. **chocolate** — sô cô la
5. **raspberry** — dâu rừng
6. **almond** — hạnh nhân
7. **coconut** — dừa
8. **coffee** — cà phê
9. **vanilla** — va ni
10. **caramel** — caramel

Q&A Pattern 1

Do you want an ice cream, too?
No, I think I'll just get some coconut water.

Q&A Pattern 2

Which flavor would you like today?
I'll have chocolate flavor and Joe would like mint flavor, please.

Q&A Pattern 3

Would you like your ice cream in a cone or in a bowl?
I'd like it in a bowl.

Conversation 1

Joe: Dad, can we get an ice cream on the way home?

Dad: Sure. Let's stop at BB's Ice Cream Shop.

Joe: Do you want an ice cream, too?

Helen: No, I think I'll just get some <u>coconut</u> water.

Dad: Are you sure? The <u>chocolate</u> ice cream there is delicious.

Helen: I know, but I'm trying to eat healthier.

Joe: <u>Cherry</u> ice cream has fruit in it. Fruit is healthy.

Helen: There's also a lot of sugar in it.

Joe: It sure does taste great, but my favorite is <u>mint</u> ice cream!

Dad: Hopefully, the shop has that flavor.

Answer the questions

1. Who asked Dad for ice cream?

2. What does Helen want to get?

3. Why doesn't Helen want to eat ice cream?

4. Which flavor does Joe like?

Put the sentences in order

Dad thinks the chocolate ice cream at BB's Ice Cream shop is delicious. ___

Joe wants to get some ice cream on the way home. (1)

Joe's favorite ice cream flavor is mint. ___

Helen doesn't want to get any ice cream. ___

Conversation 2

Bob: Welcome to BB's Ice Cream Shop.

Dad: Hi, Bob. How are things with you?

Bob: It's a hot summer, so business is excellent!

Bob: Which flavor would you like today?

Dad: I'll have chocolate flavor and Joe would like mint flavor, please.

Bob: Would you like your ice cream in a cone or in a bowl?

Joe: I'd like it in a bowl. Put some nuts on top, too.

Bob: How about you, Helen? Are you going to have strawberry flavor, again?

Helen: No, I'll have a coconut water instead.

Dad: The weather really is nice today. Let's sit outside.

Answer the questions

1. Why is business good at BB's ice cream shop?
2. Does Joe want his ice cream in a cone?
3. What does Joe want on top of his ice cream?
4. Where does Dad want to sit?

Noun, Verb or Adjective?

excellent ☐ Noun ☐ Verb ☐ ADJ

flavor ☐ Noun ☐ Verb ☐ ADJ

bowl ☐ Noun ☐ Verb ☐ ADJ

have ☐ Noun ☐ Verb ☐ ADJ

nice ☐ Noun ☐ Verb ☐ ADJ

weather ☐ Noun ☐ Verb ☐ ADJ

hot ☐ Noun ☐ Verb ☐ ADJ

like ☐ Noun ☐ Verb ☐ ADJ

Take the test

Write the answer next to the letter "A"

A: ___ 1. ___ wants to eat ice cream.

a. Dad   b. Helen   c. Joe

A: ___ 2. Dad thinks the ___ ice cream is delicious.

a. coconut   b. cherry   c. chocolate

A: ___ 3. Helen is trying to eat ___.

a. health   b. healthier   c. more healthy

A: ___ 4. "It sure does ___ great, but my favorite is mint ice cream!"

a. tasting   b. tastes   c. taste

A: ___ 5. Business at BB's Ice Cream Shop is excellent because ___.

a. the ice cream is yummy   b. there are many flavors   c. the weather is hot

A: ___ 6. Joe ordered a ___ ice cream.

a. mint   b. strawberry   c. chocolate

A: ___ 7. Joe wants to put his ice cream in a cone with nuts on top.

a. True.   b. False.   c. Not given.

A: ___ 8. Helen usually has ___ ice cream.

a. raspberry   b. cherry   c. strawberry

Answers on Page 206

Lesson 19: The weather

thời tiết

Learn the words

1. sunny
   nắng
2. rainy
   mưa rơi
3. snowy
   có tuyết rơi
4. cloudy
   có mây
5. windy
   gió
6. cold
   lạnh
7. warm
   ấm áp
8. hot
   nóng
9. freezing
   đóng băng
10. cool
    mát mẻ

Q&A Pattern 1

What does the weather forecast say?
It says there's a chance of rain, but mostly <u>cloudy</u>.

Q&A Pattern 2

What has she been doing?
She's been learning how to ski.

Q&A Pattern 3

How does she keep <u>warm</u> at night?
She keeps <u>warm</u> by sitting in front of the fireplace at the hotel.

Conversation 1

Brad: Are we still going for a bike ride tomorrow?

Tom: It depends on the weather. If it's a <u>rainy</u> day, I'd rather stay home.

Brad: It's been <u>sunny</u> all week.

Tom: I heard it's going to rain sometime this week.

Brad: What does the weather forecast say?

Tom: It says there's a chance of rain, but mostly <u>cloudy</u>.

Brad: That sounds okay. What do you think?

Tom: It depends on how <u>windy</u> it gets. It's difficult to ride in the wind.

Brad: Should we wait until the morning and then decide?

Tom: Yes, I think that would be best.

Answer the questions

1. What are the boys planning to do tomorrow?
2. How has the weather been this week?
3. What could make it difficult to ride a bike?
4. When will they decide if they can go bike riding?

Unscramble the words

1. all / sunny / week / been / weather / The / has
2. a / of / There / rain / is / chance
3. cloudy / will / forecast / The / it / weather / be / mostly / says
4. ride / the / wind / It's / to / difficult / in

Conversation 2

Tom: I got an email from Lucy today. She's having a great time in Canada.

Brad: What has she been doing?

Tom: She's been learning how to ski. Here's a photo of her skiing.

Brad: Wow! It looks like it's very snowy there right now.

Tom: Abby must be freezing.

Brad: That's true. Lucy's never been to such a cold place before.

Tom: Yes, and she's used to living in a hot place.

Brad: How does she keep warm at night?

Tom: She keeps warm by sitting in front of the fireplace at the hotel.

Brad: It sounds like she's having the best time.

Answer the questions

1. Who did Tom receive an email from?

2. What has Lucy been doing in Canada?

3. How is the weather in Canada now?

4. How does Lucy keep warm at night?

Find three nouns, verbs and adjectives

Nouns	Verbs	Adjectives
1. _____	1. _____	2. _____
2. _____	2. _____	2. _____
3. _____	3. _____	3. _____

Take the test

Write the answer next to the letter "A"

A: ___ 1. Tom would rather stay home if it's a ___ day.

a. cloudy   b. snowy   c. rainy

A: ___ 2. Tom heard it's going to rain ___ this week.

a. meantime   b. sometimes   c. sometime

A: ___ 3. "It depends ___ how windy it gets."

a. over   b. on   c. for

A: ___ 4. The boys will wait ___ the morning and then decide.

a. in   b. out   c. until

A: ___ 5. Lucy ___ a great time in Canada.

a. is having   b. had   c. has

A: ___ 6. Lucy has ___ how to ski.

a. learned   b. been learning   c. be learning

A: ___ 7. "Lucy's never ___ to such a cold place before."

a. go   b. went   c. been

A: ___ 8. Lucy is used to living in a ___ place.

a. sunny   b. hot   c. cold

Answers on Page 206

Lesson 20: In the living room

trong phòng khách

Learn the words

1. **coffee table** — bàn café
2. **armchair** — ghế bành
3. **clock** — đồng hồ
4. **television** — ti vi
5. **bookcase** — tủ sách
6. **sofa** — ghế sô pha
7. **vase** — bình hoa
8. **rug** — thảm
9. **TV stand** — giá đỡ TV
10. **painting** — bức vẽ

Q&A Pattern 1

Where did you get that <u>vase</u> from?
I got it from my mother.

Q&A Pattern 2

Do you remember the <u>rug</u> you liked at the department store?
Yes, I remember it.

Q&A Pattern 3

Where are you going to put the <u>rug</u>?
I'm going to put it under the <u>armchair</u>.

Conversation 1

Fran: I really love how you've designed your living room.

Pam: I do, too. It's nice to sit on the armchair and relax.

Fran: I notice you don't have a television.

Pam: I have one in my bedroom. I replaced the TV stand with a bookcase.

Fran: Where did you get that vase from?

Pam: I got it from my mother. She bought it for my new home.

Fran: It's really beautiful. And it looks great with the wall painting.

Pam: I like how they both have the same colors.

Fran: After seeing your living room, I want to change mine!

Pam: You should. It's an important place in the home.

Answer the questions

1. Does Pam have a television?

2. What did Pam replace the TV stand with?

3. Who gave Pam the vase?

4. What does Fran think of the vase?

Fill in the blanks

Fran: Where _____ you _____ that _____ from?

Pam: I got it _____ my _____. She _____ it for _____ new _____.

Fran: It's _____ beautiful. And it _____ great _____ the wall _____.

Pam: I like _____ they _____ have the _____ colors.

Conversation 2

Pam: I put your milk tea on the coffee table.

Fran: Thanks. I also have something special for you.

Pam: Another gift? You already got me a blender for the kitchen.

Fran: Do you remember the rug you liked at the department store?

Pam: Yes, I remember it. It was much too expensive.

Fran: I know you really wanted it, so I decided to get it for you.

Pam: Thank you so much! It's wonderful!

Fran: Where are you going to put the rug?

Pam: I'm going to put it under the sofa.

Fran: That's a good idea. It will look really great there.

Answer the questions

1. What did Pam put on the coffee table?

2. How many gifts did Fran get for Pam?

3. Why didn't Pam buy the rug?

4. Where is Pam going to put the rug?

Past, Present or Future?

1. I also have something special for you.   ☐ **Past** ☐ **Present** ☐ **Future**

2. You already got me a blender for the kitchen.   ☐ **Past** ☐ **Present** ☐ **Future**

3. I'm going to put it under the sofa.   ☐ **Past** ☐ **Present** ☐ **Future**

4. It will look really great there.   ☐ **Past** ☐ **Present** ☐ **Future**

Take the test

Write the answer next to the letter "A"

A: ___ **1.** Fran likes how Pam designed her ___.

a. living room   b. dining room   c. bedroom

A: ___ **2.** Pam doesn't have a television.

a. True.   b. False.   c. Not given.

A: ___ **3.** Pam replaced the TV stand with a ___.

a. coffee table   b. armchair   c. bookcase

A: ___ **4.** The vase was given to Pam by ___.

a. Fran   b. her mother   c. her aunt

A: ___ **5.** Fran had already given Pam a ___.

a. rug   b. blender   c. vase

A: ___ **6.** Pam didn't get the rug because it was too ___.

a. wonderful   b. expensive   c. great

A: ___ **7.** "I know you really wanted it, so I ___ to get it for you."

a. decided   b. have decided   c. decide

A: ___ **8.** Pam is going to put the rug under the ___.

a. bookcase   b. coffee table   c. sofa

Answers on Page 206

Lesson 21: Chores

việc nhà

Learn the words

1. **take out the trash**
   vứt rác
2. **wash the dishes**
   rửa bát đĩa
3. **feed the pets**
   cho thú cưng ăn
4. **vacuum the carpet**
   hút bụi thảm
5. **clean the bedroom**
   dọn phòng ngủ
6. **iron the clothes**
   ủi quần áo
7. **mop the floor**
   lau nhà
8. **cook dinner**
   nấu bữa tối
9. **do the laundry**
   giặt áo quần
10. **make the beds**
    dọn giường

Q&A Pattern 1

What would you like me to do?
You can <u>vacuum the carpet</u>.

Q&A Pattern 2

Who is going to <u>cook dinner</u>?
We may have to <u>cook dinner</u> together.

Q&A Pattern 3

Which chores do you usually do?
I usually <u>feed the pets</u>.

Conversation 1

Sean: We have to do the chores before our friends come over for dinner.

Karen: I know. We don't have much time.

Sean: I've already mopped the floor, but there's still a lot to do.

Karen: I can help. What would you like me to do?

Sean: You can vacuum the carpet. It hasn't been done for a month.

Karen: Sure, but I think I'll take out the trash first.

Sean: Good idea. The trash can is already full.

Karen: You should go to the supermarket and buy some meat and vegetables.

Sean: Who is going to cook dinner?

Karen: We may have to cook dinner together so that it's ready on time.

Answer the questions

1. Who will be coming over for dinner?
2. What has Sean already done?
3. How long hasn't the carpet been vacuumed?
4. Where is Sean about to go?

True or False?

1. Sean and Karen's friends will be coming over for dinner. ☐ **True** ☐ **False**

2. Sean hasn't mopped the floor yet. ☐ **True** ☐ **False**

3. The floor hasn't been vacuumed for a week. ☐ **True** ☐ **False**

4. They will cook dinner together. ☐ **True** ☐ **False**

Conversation 2

Paul: Thanks for inviting us over for dinner.

Karen: It's no problem. Thank you for coming.

Jane: The meal is delicious. Karen, I didn't know you were such a good cook.

Karen: Sean helped me <u>cook dinner</u> as well.

Paul: Sean looks tired today. Have you been working a lot?

Sean: No, it's been a busy day. Karen and I have been cleaning the house.

Jane: Which chores do you usually do?

Sean: I usually <u>feed the pets</u>. Karen <u>does the laundry</u> and <u>irons the clothes</u>.

Karen: Recently, the children have started to <u>make the beds</u> in their rooms.

Paul: One day, they might even <u>clean their bedrooms</u>!

Answer the questions

1. What does Jane think about the meal?

2. Why does Sean look tired?

3. Does Karen feed the pets?

4. What have Karen and Paul's children started to do?

Write the adjectives

1. Jane thinks the meal is _____ .

2. Jane didn't know Karen was such a _____ cook.

3. Paul thinks Sean looks _____ today.

4. Sean has had a _____ day.

Take the test

Write the answer next to the letter "A"

A: ___ **1.** They have to do the chores ___ their friends come for dinner.

a. when   b. after   c. before

A: ___ **2.** Sean has already ___.

a. cooked dinner   b. mopped the floor   c. vacuumed the carpet

A: ___ **3.** Karen wanted to ___ out the trash first.

a. taken   b. took   c. take

A: ___ **4.** Who is going to cook dinner?

a. Sean.   b. Karen.   c. Sean and Karen.

A: ___ **5.** "Karen, I didn't know you were ___ a good cook."

a. very   b. such   c. much

A: ___ **6.** Sean is tired because he has been ___.

a. cleaning the house   b. working a lot   c. cooking dinner

A: ___ **7.** Karen usually ___ the laundry.

a. irons   b. makes   c. does

A: ___ **8.** The children have recently started to ___.

a. make the beds   b. clean the bedroom   c. feed the pets

Answers on Page 206

Lesson 22: Pets

vật nuôi

Learn the words

1. rabbit
   thỏ
2. cat
   mèo
3. dog
   chó
4. guinea pig
   chuột bạch
5. bird
   chim
6. fish
   cá
7. turtle
   rùa
8. mouse
   chuột
9. hamster
   chuột hamster
10. snake
    rắn

Q&A Pattern 1

Do you have any pets?
Yes, I have one <u>cat</u> and two <u>fish</u>.

Q&A Pattern 2

What do you feed the <u>rabbit</u>?
I mostly feed it fruit.

Q&A Pattern 3

Doesn't he have a <u>turtle</u>?
Yes, he does.

Conversation 1

Ben: Do you have any pets?

Kate: Yes, I have one cat and two mice.

Ben: Are the mice worried about the cat wanting to eat them?

Kate: Yes, they are. I never take the mice out to play when the cat is around.

Ben: We have a rabbit and it gets along well with the dog.

Kate: That's interesting. Your dog is very friendly.

Ben: That's true. They play with each other all day.

Kate: What do you feed the rabbit?

Ben: I mostly feed it fruit. It also likes green leafy vegetables.

Kate: That's similar to a hamster I used to have.

Answer the questions

1. How many mice does Kate have?
2. Does Kate let the cat play with the mice?
3. What is Ben's dog like?
4. What does Ben feed the rabbit?

Complete the sentences using three words

1. Kate never takes the mice out when the _____.
2. The rabbit gets along well _____.
3. Ben's dog _____.
4. Ben feeds the rabbit fruit and _____.

Conversation 2

Mom: We are going on our trip to Europe next week.

Ben: Have you found someone who can look after Floppy?

Mom: No, not yet. Janet offered to help, but she has a very big <u>dog</u>.

Ben: We have to be careful. Some <u>dogs</u> might hurt a <u>rabbit</u>.

Mom: How about David? Doesn't he have a <u>turtle</u>?

Ben: Yes, he does. He also has a pet <u>snake</u>. David loves reptiles.

Mom: I'm not sure if I feel comfortable leaving Floppy with a <u>snake</u>.

Ben: The neighbor only has <u>fish</u>. We could ask him.

Mom: That's a good idea. I'm sure Derek won't mind.

Ben: He likes <u>rabbits</u>, too. He sometimes feeds Floppy food from his garden.

Answer the questions

1. Where are they going on a trip to next week?

2. Why doesn't Mom want to leave the rabbit with David?

3. What kind of pet does Derek have?

4. Who will they ask to look after the rabbit?

Which person?

1. _____ offered to help look after Floppy, but has a very big dog.

2. _____ loves reptiles and has a pet snake.

3. _____ has fish and likes rabbits.

4. _____ wants to ask the neighbor to look after Floppy.

Take the test

Write the answer next to the letter "A"

A: ___ **1.** How many mice does Kate have?

a. One.　　　　　　　　b. Two.　　　　　　　　c. Three.

A: ___ **2.** Kate never takes the mice ___ when the cat is ___.

a. about, in　　　　　　b. around, out　　　　　c. out, around

A: ___ **3.** Ben's rabbit gets along with the ___.

a. cat　　　　　　　　　b. dog　　　　　　　　　c. hamster

A: ___ **4.** Ben feeds his pet green leafy ___.

a. vegetables　　　　　b. fruit　　　　　　　　c. leaves

A: ___ **5.** Floppy is a ___.

a. dog　　　　　　　　　b. rabbit　　　　　　　c. turtle

A: ___ **6.** Ben doesn't feel comfortable leaving Floppy with David because he has a ___.

a. reptile　　　　　　　b. turtle　　　　　　　c. snake

A: ___ **7.** Who will Ben ask to look after his pet?

a. David.　　　　　　　b. Derek.　　　　　　　c. Kate.

A: ___ **8.** Which pet was not mentioned?

a. A guinea pig.　　　b. A snake.　　　　　　c. A hamster.

Answers on Page 206

Lesson 23 — Skills

kỹ năng

Learn the words

1. swim
   bơi lội
2. ski
   trượt tuyết
3. sing
   hát
4. draw
   vẽ tranh
5. read
   đọc
6. cook
   nấu ăn
7. surf
   lướt sóng
8. ride
   lái
9. write
   viết
10. run
    chạy

Q&A Pattern 1

What do you want to learn to do?
I want to learn how to surf.

Q&A Pattern 2

What did you do in the evenings?
I did a lot of reading.

Q&A Pattern 3

Can you teach me how to surf this summer?
Yes, I can.

Conversation 1

Brad: How was your trip to Canada?

Lucy: It was amazing. It's a beautiful country.

Brad: I saw a photo of you learning how to <u>ski</u>.

Lucy: Yes, it was so much fun!

Brad: I'd like to learn a new skill one day.

Lucy: What do you want to learn to do?

Brad: I want to learn how to <u>surf</u>. It's a great outdoor activity to do in summer.

Lucy: I enjoyed <u>skiing</u> very much, but the weather is really cold in winter.

Brad: What did you do in the evenings?

Lucy: I did a lot of <u>reading</u>. It was nice to <u>read</u> a book in front of the fireplace.

Answer the questions

1. What did Brad see a photograph of?
2. Which skill did Lucy learn how to do?
3. When does Brad want to learn to surf?
4. What did Lucy do in the evenings?

Put the sentences in order

Brad wants to learn how to surf. ___

Lucy read a book in front of the fireplace in the evenings. ___

Brad saw a photograph of Lucy learning how to ski. ___

Lucy's trip to Canada was amazing. (1)

Conversation 2

Brad: Can you teach me how to surf this summer?

Tom: Yes, I can. You need to be a strong swimmer.

Brad: I know how to swim. I learned how when I was six years old.

Tom: I think you should practice more before you go surfing.

Brad: No problem. I'll start practicing on the weekends.

Tom: Good. Now, let's prepare dinner. Mom asked me to cook spaghetti.

Brad: She wrote down the recipe and left it on the table.

Tom: Yes, I saw that. The problem is we don't have any pasta sauce.

Brad: I can run down to the shop and get some.

Tom: Take my bike. You'll get there quicker if you ride.

Answer the questions

1. When did Brad learn how to swim?
2. What are the boys going to cook?
3. What do they need to buy for dinner?
4. How will Brad go to the shop?

Noun, Verb or Adjective?

problem ☐ Noun ☐ Verb ☐ ADJ   **know** ☐ Noun ☐ Verb ☐ ADJ

learned ☐ Noun ☐ Verb ☐ ADJ   **dinner** ☐ Noun ☐ Verb ☐ ADJ

practicing ☐ Noun ☐ Verb ☐ ADJ   **think** ☐ Noun ☐ Verb ☐ ADJ

sauce ☐ Noun ☐ Verb ☐ ADJ   **strong** ☐ Noun ☐ Verb ☐ ADJ

Take the test

Write the answer next to the letter "A"

A: ___ **1.** Lucy was learning how to ___ in Canada.

a. surf   b. swim   c. ski

A: ___ **2.** Brad would like to learn how to ___.

a. ski   b. surf   c. cook

A: ___ **3.** Lucy thought the weather in Canada was very cold in ___.

a. autumn   b. winter   c. summer

A: ___ **4.** "It was nice to read a book ___ front of the fireplace."

a. in   b. by   c. on

A: ___ **5.** Tom wants Brad to practice ___.

a. surfing   b. swimming   c. running

A: ___ **6.** Mom's recipe for spaghetti is the boys' favorite.

a. True   b. False   c. Not given

A: ___ **7.** The boys don't have any ___ for the spaghetti.

a. pasta   b. pasta sauce   c. meat

A: ___ **8.** Brad is going to ___ to the supermarket.

a. run   b. ride   c. walk

Answers on Page 206

Lesson 24 — Meats

thịt

Learn the words

1. beef
   thịt bò
2. fish
   cá
3. pork
   thịt heo
4. salami
   xúc xích Ý
5. bacon
   Thịt ba rọi
6. chicken
   thịt gà
7. sausage
   Lạp xưởng
8. lamb
   cừu
9. shrimp
   tôm
10. ham
    giăm bông

Q&A Pattern 1

What would you like to eat for breakfast?
I would like to have some <u>bacon</u> and eggs.

Q&A Pattern 2

Do we have any <u>ham</u>?
Yes, we do.

Q&A Pattern 3

What kind of sandwiches did you make?
I made some <u>beef</u> sandwiches.

Conversation 1

Mom: What would you like to eat for breakfast?

Abby: I would like to have some bacon and eggs.

Mom: We don't have any bacon left, but you can have a sausage instead.

Abby: I don't feel like eating a sausage. Do we have any ham?

Mom: Yes, we do. I'll put it on a toast.

Abby: Thank you. I better eat it quickly. I only have ten minutes.

Mom: Are you still going fishing with Grandpa this morning?

Abby: Yes, I am. We're going out on the boat today.

Mom: That sounds like fun. Grandpa must be very excited.

Abby: I'm excited, too. Hopefully, I'll catch a big fish!

Answer the questions

1. What does Abby not want to eat?
2. What is Mom going to put the ham on?
3. How long does Abby have to eat breakfast?
4. What is Abby going to do today?

Unscramble the words

1. eat / eggs / bacon / to / Abby / like / and / would
2. feel / sausage / Abby / a / eating / like / doesn't
3. has / minutes / Abby / ten / only
4. boat / the / fishing / today / going / They're / on

Conversation 2

Abby: Thank you for taking me out fishing on the boat.

Grandpa: You are very welcome! This is a lot of fun.

Abby: What are we using as bait today?

Grandpa: We are using shrimp. The fish love to eat it.

Abby: If you're hungry, there are some sandwiches in the lunchbox.

Grandpa: I am hungry. What kind of sandwiches did you make?

Abby: I made some beef sandwiches. I know they're your favorite.

Grandpa: Yes, they are. Here's your chicken sandwich.

Abby: Wait! I think I have a fish on my line.

Grandpa: Yes, you do. Look in the water. It's a huge one!

Answer the questions

1. What are they using as bait?

2. What is Grandpa's favorite sandwich?

3. Which meat was put in Abby's sandwich?

4. How big is the fish on Abby's fishing line?

Find three nouns, verbs and adjectives

Nouns	Verbs	Adjectives
1. _____	1. _____	2. _____
2. _____	2. _____	2. _____
3. _____	3. _____	3. _____

Take the test

Write the answer next to the letter "A"

A: ___ **1.** Abby wanted some ___ and eggs.

a. bacon					b. sausage					c. salami

A: ___ **2.** What did Mom put on Abby's toast?

a. ham					b. bacon					c. sausage

A: ___ **3.** Abby only ___ ten minutes to eat breakfast.

a. having					b. have					c. has

A: ___ **4.** Abby will be going fishing with her ___.

a. grandmother				b. father					c. grandfather

A: ___ **5.** The fish love to eat ___.

a. bait					b. shrimp					c. sausage

A: ___ **6.** "If you're hungry, there ___ some sandwiches in the lunchbox."

a. are					b. is						c. have

A: ___ **7.** ___ sandwiches are Grandpa's favorite.

a. Salami					b. Ham					c. Beef

A: ___ **8.** Abby has ___ in her sandwich.

a. chicken					b. beef					c. fish

Answers on Page 206

Lesson 25 Countries

quốc gia

Learn the words

1. **Canada**
   Canada
2. **Brazil**
   Bra-xin
3. **Japan**
   Nhật Bản
4. **Australia**
   Australia
5. **South Africa**
   Nam Phi
6. **Mexico**
   Mexico
7. **Germany**
   Đức
8. **China**
   Trung Quốc
9. **Russia**
   Nga
10. **England**
    nước Anh

Q&A Pattern 1

Have you thought about studying in <u>Canada</u>?

Yes, I have.

Q&A Pattern 2

Is <u>England</u> too far to travel to?

Yes, it's a little too far.

Q&A Pattern 3

What about <u>Germany</u>?

<u>Germany</u> always has a chance to win.

Conversation 1

Mika: I'm thinking about studying abroad.

Nico: I think that would be great. Which country do you want to go to?

Mika: I would like to go to an English-speaking country.

Nico: A lot of people from <u>Japan</u> study at a university in <u>Australia</u>.

Mika: I have a friend from <u>China</u> there and she loves it.

Nico: Have you thought about studying in <u>Canada</u>?

Mika: Yes, I have. It's very far from <u>Japan</u>.

Nico: Is <u>England</u> too far to travel to?

Mika: Yes, it's a little too far. It would be an interesting place to study.

Nico: Yes, there are a lot of great countries to consider.

Answer the questions

1. What is Mika thinking about doing?

2. What kind of country does she want to study in?

3. Where does Mika's friend in Australia come from?

4. What does Mika think about Canada?

Fill in the blanks

Nico: A lot of _____ from _____ study at a _____ in _____.

Mika: I have a _____ from China _____ and she _____ it.

Nico: Have you _____ about _____ in _____?

Mika: Yes, I _____. It's very _____ from _____.

Conversation 2

Nico: Who do you think will win the World Cup in soccer?

Mika: It's difficult to say. I don't think <u>Japan</u> will do well.

Nico: My friend from <u>Russia</u> thinks <u>Brazil</u> will win.

Mika: I'm not sure if they will. There are many good teams this time.

Nico: That's true. Even <u>England</u> has a chance.

Mika: I agree. They did very well in Europe recently.

Nico: European teams are always good. What about <u>Germany</u>?

Mika: <u>Germany</u> always has a chance to win.

Nico: I watched them play <u>Mexico</u> last week. Both teams played well.

Mika: It's definitely going to be an exciting competition.

Answer the questions

1. Does Mika think Japan will do well at the World Cup?

2. Which country does Nico's friend from Russia think will win?

3. Why does Mika agree that England has a chance to win?

4. Which two countries played soccer last week?

Past or Present?

1. There are many good teams this time.   ☐ Past ☐ Present

2. They did very well in Europe recently.   ☐ Past ☐ Present

3. European teams are always good.   ☐ Past ☐ Present

4. I watched them play Mexico last week.   ☐ Past ☐ Present

Take the test

Write the answer next to the letter "A"

A: ___ **1.** Mika is thinking about ___ abroad.

a. studies	b. study	c. studying

A: ___ **2.** Mika's friend from ___ loves studying in Australia.

a. Japan	b. China	c. Brazil

A: ___ **3.** There are a lot of ___ countries to consider.

a. far	b. great	c. interesting

A: ___ **4.** Which country is Mika from?

a. Japan.	b. England.	c. China.

A: ___ **5.** Nico's friend from Russia thinks ___ will win the World Cup.

a. Russia	b. Brazil	c. England

A: ___ **6.** Does Mika think England has a chance to win the World Cup?

a. Yes, she does.	b. No, she doesn't.	c. She is not sure.

A: ___ **7.** Nico thought ___ played well.

a. Mexico	b. Germany	c. both teams

A: ___ **8.** Mika thinks the World Cup will be ___.

a. interesting	b. great	c. exciting

Answers on Page 206

Lesson 26 — Languages

ngôn ngữ

Learn the words

1. **English**
   tiếng anh
2. **German**
   tiếng đức
3. **Portuguese**
   tiếng bồ đào nha
4. **Japanese**
   tiếng nhật
5. **Vietnamese**
   tiếng việt
6. **Spanish**
   tiếng tây ban nha
7. **French**
   tiếng pháp
8. **Chinese**
   tiếng trung quốc
9. **Hindi**
   tiếng hindi
10. **Arabic**
    tiếng ả rập

Q&A Pattern 1

Does Kim speak Vietnamese in Australia?
Yes, she does.

Q&A Pattern 2

Are you still studying German?
Yes, I am.

Q&A Pattern 3

Which language do you want to learn?
I want to learn Spanish.

Conversation 1

Nico: Have you decided where you want to study abroad?

Mika: Yes, I have. I will go to Australia.

Nico: My friend, Lin, lives there and loves it. Why did you choose this place?

Mika: Many students from Japan study there. I can use Japanese sometimes.

Nico: Lin told me she gets tired of speaking English all day.

Mika: Does Lin speak Chinese in Australia?

Nico: Yes, she does. There are lot of immigrants from China there.

Mika: I assume many people speak Vietnamese as well.

Nico: Yes, there are. You'll hear a lot of different languages spoken there.

Mika: When I visited Melbourne, I heard many people speaking Arabic, too.

Answer the questions

1. Which country will Mika study abroad in?

2. Who lives in Australia now?

3. Why does Lin sometimes speak Chinese?

4. Which city did Mika visit in Australia?

True or False?

1. Mika has decided to study in Australia.   ☐ **True** ☐ **False**

2. Lin sometimes speaks Japanese in Australia.   ☐ **True** ☐ **False**

3. A lot of Chinese people migrate to Australia.   ☐ **True** ☐ **False**

4. Mika has never been to Melbourne.   ☐ **True** ☐ **False**

Conversation 2

Nico: Hi, Lin. Please excuse my poor English.

Lin: Thank you for calling. Your English is actually pretty good!

Nico: I have a friend named Mika who wants to study in Australia.

Lin: Great! If she has any questions, she can ask me.

Nico: I will tell her. I'm sure she will have many questions.

Lin: Are you still studying German?

Nico: Not anymore. It was too difficult. I want to study a new language.

Lin: Which language do you want to learn?

Nico: I want to learn Spanish. I heard it's easier than German.

Lin: I once tried to study French. It's also a difficult language to learn.

Answer the questions

1. How did Nico describe his English ability?

2. Why did Nico stop learning German?

3. Which language does Nico want to study?

4. Which language did Lin find difficult to learn?

Write the verbs

1. Mika wants to _____ in Australia.

2. If Mika has any questions, she can _____ Lin.

3. Nico _____ Spanish is easier to learn than German.

4. Lin once _____ to study French.

Take the test

Write the answer next to the letter "A"

A: ___ **1.** Mika has decided to study in ___.

a. England b. Australia c. New Zealand

A: ___ **2.** Mika can sometimes speak ___ with her friends while studying abroad.

a. Chinese b. German c. Japanese

A: ___ **3.** Nico's friend, Lin, gets tired of speaking ___ all day.

a. Chinese b. Japanese c. English

A: ___ **4.** A lot of different languages ___ in Melbourne.

a. are speaking b. are spoken c. being speak

A: ___ **5.** "The best way to learn a language is to live in the place where it is ___."

a. spoken b. speaks c. speaking

A: ___ **6.** Nico is no longer studying ___.

a. German b. Spanish c. Arabic

A: ___ **7.** Nico heard it's easier to learn ___ than German.

a. French b. English c. Spanish

A: ___ **8.** Lin found it ___ to learn French.

a. easy b. difficult c. quick

Answers on Page 206

Lesson 27 — In the refrigerator

trong tủ lạnh

Learn the words

1. milk
   sữa
2. meat
   thịt
3. bread
   bánh mỳ
4. ice
   đá
5. water
   nước
6. cola
   cô ca
7. tea
   trà
8. salad
   sa lát
9. juice
   nước ép
10. ice cream
    kem

Q&A Pattern 1

What should I put on the shopping list?
Put <u>bread</u> on the shopping list.

Q&A Pattern 2

Can you get some orange <u>juice</u>?
Yes, I can.

Q&A Pattern 3

Should we get a <u>salad</u> for lunch?
I think that's a good idea.

Conversation 1

Dad: I'm going to the supermarket. What should I put on the shopping list?

Mom: Put bread on the shopping list. We ran out this morning.

Helen: Get some almond milk again. It tastes pretty good.

Joe: I want some cola. Get a big bottle this time.

Dad: No, Joe. You've been drinking too many sugar drinks.

Mom: You also ate too much ice cream. There's nothing left.

Joe: It wasn't just me. Helen ate some as well.

Helen: I only had one bowl of ice cream. You ate the rest!

Joe: I don't want to drink water all day. Can you get some orange juice?

Dad: Yes, I can. That's much healthier than cola.

Answer the questions

1. What kind of milk does Helen want?
2. Will Dad buy some cola for Joe?
3. How many bowls of ice cream did Helen eat?
4. Which drink will Dad get for Joe?

Complete the sentences using three words

1. Mom wants Dad to put bread on _____.
2. Helen thinks almond milk _____.
3. Joe has been drinking too _____.
4. Orange juice is much _____.

Conversation 2

Dad: Thanks for coming to the supermarket with me.

Helen: You're welcome. Let me look at the shopping list.

Dad: Let's get some <u>bread</u> first. What kind do you want?

Helen: My favorite is multigrain, but Joe likes white <u>bread</u>.

Dad: We can get both. Hey, look at these different <u>salads</u>. They look yummy.

Helen: I agree. Should we get a <u>salad</u> for lunch?

Dad: I think that's a good idea. Does any of them have <u>meat</u>?

Helen: Yes, this one has chicken. We can buy this one.

Dad: Great. Let's get some lemon <u>tea</u> for Mom. Do we have <u>ice</u> at home?

Helen: Yes, we do. Mom's favorite is the one on the top shelf.

Answer the questions

1. Where are they now?
2. Which bread does Joe like to eat?
3. What are they going to have for lunch?
4. What kind of tea did they get for Mom?

Which person?

1. _____ likes white bread.
2. _____ wants to look at the shopping list.
3. _____ thinks the salads look yummy.
4. _____ likes the lemon tea on the top shelf.

Take the test

Write the answer next to the letter "A"

A: ___ **1.** What did Mom tell Dad to put on the shopping list?

a. Bread. b. Ice cream. c. Milk.

A: ___ **2.** The bread ran ___ this morning.

a. off b. out c. up

A: ___ **3.** Joe has been eating too much ___.

a. ice cream b. white bread c. cola

A: ___ **4.** Joe ___ want to drink water all day.

a. hasn't b. doesn't c. don't

A: ___ **5.** Who went to the supermarket with Dad?

a. Mom. b. Joe. c. Helen.

A: ___ **6.** They decided to get the salad that has chicken in it.

a. True. b. False. c. Not given.

A: ___ **7.** Do they have ice at home?

a. Yes, they do. b. No, they don't. c. Helen is not sure.

A: ___ **8.** Mom's favorite lemon tea is on the ___ shelf.

a. bottom b. middle c. top

Answers on Page 206

Lesson 28: Desserts

món tráng miệng

Learn the words

1. **ice cream**
   kem
2. **apple pie**
   bánh táo
3. **cheesecake**
   bánh pho mát
4. **pudding**
   bánh pudding
5. **cake**
   bánh ngọt
6. **cupcakes**
   bánh cupcake
7. **brownies**
   bánh brownie
8. **pastries**
   bánh ngọt
9. **waffles**
   bánh quế
10. **cookies**
    bánh quy

Q&A Pattern 1

How are the <u>brownies</u> at this place?
They are too sweet for me.

Q&A Pattern 2

What are you going to have for dessert?
My son wants to have <u>ice cream</u>.

Q&A Pattern 3

What kind of <u>cake</u> are you thinking about getting?
I'm thinking about getting a <u>cheesecake</u>.

Conversation 1

Janet: Thanks for meeting me at the café. Do you want to order some food?

Sam: I've already had lunch, so I won't have anything.

Janet: I think I'll have something. How are the brownies at this place?

Sam: They are too sweet for me. Perhaps you should get cookies instead.

Janet: They've sold out of them. Do you have any other suggestions?

Sam: You should try the apple pie. It's delicious.

Janet: I ate one for dessert last night. I don't want to eat it again.

Sam: Those pastries look pretty good.

Janet: I agree. Are you sure you don't want one?

Sam: I think I'll change my mind. Get me one with cream on top.

Answer the questions

1. Why doesn't Sam like the brownies at the café?

2. Why can't Janet get some cookies?

3. What did Janet eat last night for dessert?

4. What does Sam want on his pastry?

Put the sentences in order

Sam has already eaten lunch today. (1)

Janet ate an apple pie last night for dessert. ___

The café has sold out of cookies. ___

Sam decided to get a pastry with cream on top. ___

Conversation 2

Sam: I better go home. My wife asked me to pick up dessert on the way.

Janet: What are you going to have for dessert?

Sam: My son wants to have <u>ice cream</u>.

Janet: The temperature is a bit cold for <u>ice cream</u>. Maybe <u>pudding</u> is better.

Sam: I agree. There's a bakery around the corner that has yummy <u>cakes</u>.

Janet: I know that place. My husband likes the <u>waffles</u> there.

Sam: I haven't tried them, but I know their <u>cupcakes</u> are the best.

Janet: What kind of <u>cake</u> are you thinking about getting?

Sam: I'm thinking about getting a <u>cheesecake</u>.

Janet: That's my favorite. I might get one, too.

Answer the questions

1. What does Sam's son want to eat for dessert?

2. Why does Janet think Sam shouldn't get ice cream?

3. What does Janet's husband like at the bakery?

4. What kind of cake is Sam thinking about getting?

Noun, Verb or Adjective?

agree ☐ Noun ☐ Verb ☐ ADJ

dessert ☐ Noun ☐ Verb ☐ ADJ

best ☐ Noun ☐ Verb ☐ ADJ

bakery ☐ Noun ☐ Verb ☐ ADJ

yummy ☐ Noun ☐ Verb ☐ ADJ

husband ☐ Noun ☐ Verb ☐ ADJ

tried ☐ Noun ☐ Verb ☐ ADJ

cold ☐ Noun ☐ Verb ☐ ADJ

Take the test

Write the answer next to the letter "A"

A: ___ **1.** Sam has already eaten ___.

a. breakfast   b. lunch   c. dinner

A: ___ **2.** Sam thinks the brownies are ___.

a. pretty good   b. delicious   c. too sweet

A: ___ **3.** The café has sold out of ___.

a. cookies   b. brownies   c. cupcakes

A: ___ **4.** Sam suggests Jane should try the ___.

a. pastry   b. apple pie   c. cake

A: ___ **5.** Janet thinks the weather is too cold for ice cream.

a. True.   b. False.   c. Not given.

A: ___ **6.** Janet's husband ___ the waffles at the bakery.

a. liking   b. likes   c. like

A: ___ **7.** Sam hasn't tried the ___ at the bakery.

a. brownies   b. pastries   c. waffles

A: ___ **8.** Sam is thinking about getting a ___.

a. cake   b. cheesecake   c. cupcake

Answers on Page 206

Lesson 29: At school

ở trường

Learn the words

1. **classroom** — lớp học
2. **nurse's office** — phòng y tá
3. **hall** — đại sảnh
4. **gym** — phòng thể dục
5. **office** — văn phòng
6. **computer lab** — phòng máy tính
7. **music room** — phòng âm nhạc
8. **lunchroom** — phòng ăn trưa
9. **science lab** — phòng thí nghiệm khoa học
10. **art room** — phòng nghệ thuật

Q&A Pattern 1

Where were you this morning?
I was in the <u>nurse's office</u>.

Q&A Pattern 2

Have you seen the new <u>computer lab</u>?
No, I haven't been there yet.

Q&A Pattern 3

Is your violin still in the <u>music room</u>?
No, it's in the <u>office</u> now.

Conversation 1

Jay: I didn't see you in the hall. Where were you this morning?

Mary: I was in the nurse's office.

Jay: Did something happen to you?

Mary: No, I took Susan there. She fell over in the gym and hurt her arm.

Jay: I hope she's okay. Did the nurse put a bandage on it?

Mary: Yes, she did. Susan's now resting in the classroom.

Jay: Is Susan still coming to art class today?

Mary: Yes, but I will help her carry her books to the art room.

Jay: We should leave now. The art room is far away from the classroom.

Mary: You're right. Let's go.

Answer the questions

1. Where was Mary this morning?
2. Where did Susan hurt her arm?
3. What did the nurse do?
4. How is Mary going to help Susan?

Unscramble the words

1. see / hall / Jay / the / in / Mary / didn't
2. this / nurse's / morning / the / was / office / Mary / in
3. the / gym / in / over / Susan / fell
4. from / away / room / classroom / far / art / The / is / the

Conversation 2

Susan: Thank you for meeting me in the <u>classroom</u>.

Mary: It's no problem. You can't carry your schoolbag with your injury.

Jay: How did you hurt your arm?

Susan: I was playing basketball in the <u>gym</u> and fell over.

Jay: Luckily, we only have art and computer class this afternoon.

Susan: Have you seen the new <u>computer lab</u>?

Jay: No, I haven't been there yet. Have you?

Susan: Yes, I have. It looks much better than before.

Mary: Is your violin still in the <u>music room</u>?

Susan: No, it's in the <u>office</u> now. The nurse helped me put it there.

Answer the questions

1. What was Susan doing when she fell over?

2. Which classes do they have this afternoon?

3. What does Susan think about the new computer lab?

4. Where is Susan's violin now?

Find three nouns, verbs and adjectives

Nouns	Verbs	Adjectives
1. _____	1. _____	2. _____
2. _____	2. _____	2. _____
3. _____	3. _____	3. _____

Take the test

Write the answer next to the letter "A"

A: ___ **1.** Mary was in the ___ this morning.

a. music roomb. science labc. nurse's office

A: ___ **2.** Susan fell over and hurt her arm in the ___.

a. classroomb. gymc. art room

A: ___ **3.** Mary will help carry Susan's ___ to the art room.

a. booksb. bandagec. violin

A: ___ **4.** The art room is far away from the ___.

a. gymb. nurse's officec. classroom

A: ___ **5.** Susan was playing ___ when she fell over.

a. basketballb. badmintonc. volleyball

A: ___ **6.** Has Joe seen the computer lab yet?

a. No, he hasn't.b. No, he doesn't.c. No, he didn't.

A: ___ **7.** Susan thinks the computer lab looks ___ than before.

a. more goodb. the bestc. much better

A: ___ **8.** Susan's ___ is in the office.

a. bookb. violinc. schoolbag

Answers on Page 206

Lesson 30: Transportion

vận chuyển

Learn the words

1. **ride a motorcycle**
   lái xe mô tô
2. **take an airplane**
   đi máy bay
3. **take the ferry**
   đi phà
4. **take a taxi**
   đi taxi
5. **catch a bus**
   bắt xe buýt
6. **ride a bike**
   đi xe đạp
7. **take the subway**
   đi tàu điện ngầm
8. **ride a scooter**
   đi xe scooter
9. **drive a car**
   lái xe
10. **take a train**
    lên tàu

Q&A Pattern 1

What's the best way to get to the city?
The best way is to catch a bus to the city.

Q&A Pattern 2

How did you come here?
I took a train here.

Q&A Pattern 3

How do you usually get around your town?
I usually ride a motorcycle.

Conversation 1

Greg: How do you like your new job in the city?

Pam: I love it. Living in the city is great, too!

Greg: Are you able to walk to the office from your new home?

Pam: No, but it's easy to <u>ride a bike</u> from where I live.

Greg: You also have the subway station down the road.

Pam: That's right. I <u>take the subway</u> when it rains.

Greg: My brother lives in the city and <u>rides a scooter</u> to get around.

Pam: That's a good idea. When are you coming to visit me?

Greg: I can come next Sunday. What's the best way to get to the city?

Pam: The best way is to <u>catch a bus</u> to the city.

Answer the questions

1. Does Pam like living in the city?
2. How does Pam go to work when it rains?
3. How does Greg's brother get around the city?
4. When can Greg visit Pam?

Fill in the blanks

Greg: How _____ you _____ your new _____ in the _____?

Pam: I _____ it. _____ in _____ city is _____, too!

Greg: Are you _____ to _____ to the office _____ your new _____?

Pam: No, _____ it's _____ to ride a _____ from _____ I live.

Conversation 2

Pam: How was the bus ride here?

Greg: I decided not to <u>catch a bus</u>. It would have been too slow.

Pam: Is that because of the heavy traffic today?

Greg: Yes, I would have been an hour late.

Pam: How did you come here?

Greg: I <u>took a train</u> here. It was much quicker.

Pam: How do you usually get around the town where you live?

Greg: I usually <u>ride a motorcycle</u>. The roads are much safer than in the city.

Pam: We won't have to use the roads today. We'll be <u>taking the ferry</u> instead.

Greg: Fantastic! I've always wanted to see the city from the river.

Answer the questions

1. Why didn't Greg catch a bus to the city?

2. How did Greg get to the city?

3. How does Greg usually get around the town where he lives?

4. Why is Greg happy they'll be taking the ferry today?

Past, Present or Future?

1. I decided not to catch a bus.   ☐ **Past** ☐ **Present** ☐ **Future**

2. I took a train here.   ☐ **Past** ☐ **Present** ☐ **Future**

3. The roads are much safer than in the city.   ☐ **Past** ☐ **Present** ☐ **Future**

4. We won't have to use the roads today.   ☐ **Past** ☐ **Present** ☐ **Future**

Take the test

Write the answer next to the letter "A"

A: ___ **1.** What can Pam not do to get to work?

a. Take the subway.　　　　b. Walk.　　　　c. Ride a bike.

A: ___ **2.** Pam ___ when it rains.

a. drives a car　　　　b. takes the subway　　　　c. takes a taxi

A: ___ **3.** Greg's brother ___ a scooter to get around the city.

a. rides　　　　b. takes　　　　c. drives

A: ___ **4.** Greg can visit Pam in the city next ___.

a. Friday　　　　b. Saturday　　　　c. Sunday

A: ___ **5.** Greg decided to catch a bus to the city because of the heavy traffic.

a. True.　　　　b. False.　　　　c. Not given.

A: ___ **6.** Greg would have been an hour late if he had ___.

a. taken a train　　　　b. driven a car　　　　c. caught a bus

A: ___ **7.** "The roads are much ___ than in the city."

a. more safe　　　　b. safest　　　　c. safer

A: ___ **8.** Today, they'll be taking the ___.

a. ferry　　　　b. train　　　　c. subway

Answers on Page 206

Lesson 31 — Fast food

thức ăn nhanh

Learn the words

1. a cheeseburger
   bánh burger phô mai
2. onion rings
   hành tây chiên
3. fried chicken
   gà rán
4. chicken nuggets
   gà chiên viên
5. french fries
   khoai tây chiên
6. a taco
   taco
7. a burrito
   burrito
8. a pancake
   bánh kếp
9. a doughnut
   bánh đô-nút
10. a hot dog
    xúc xích

Q&A Pattern 1

What do you want to eat?
I'll get some <u>fried chicken</u>.

Q&A Pattern 2

Have you eaten dinner yet?
Yes, I had a <u>hot dog</u>.

Q&A Pattern 3

Is there anything to eat in the kitchen?
There are some <u>doughnuts</u>.

Conversation 1

Mom: Your father and I are off to the game. You can order takeout for dinner.

Joe: Sure. I'll order some food online. What do you want to eat?

Helen: I'll get some fried chicken. Order it from Charlie's Chicken.

Joe: They also have chicken nuggets. Do you want them instead?

Helen: No, but I'll have some french fries as well.

Joe: No problem. I think I'm going to order some Mexican food.

Helen: You always get tacos. You should try something new.

Joe: Mexican food is my favorite!

Helen: You should get a burrito instead. They are delicious.

Joe: Okay, I'll get one of those. I think I'll also order some onion rings.

Answer the questions

1. What did Helen order for dinner?

2. What is Joe's favorite food?

3. What did Helen suggest Joe should get?

4. Did Joe order some french fries for himself?

True or False?

1. Mom and Dad are going to order takeout for dinner. ☐ **True** ☐ **False**

2. Helen got some french fries with her fried chicken. ☐ **True** ☐ **False**

3. Charlie's Chicken has chicken nuggets. ☐ **True** ☐ **False**

4. Joe decided to get a taco instead of a burrito. ☐ **True** ☐ **False**

Conversation 2

Joe: How was the basketball game?

Dad: We had a good time even though our team lost.

Helen: We watched the game on TV. It was exciting at the end.

Joe: Have you eaten dinner yet?

Mom: Yes, I had a <u>hot dog</u>. I'm still a little hungry.

Dad: Me, too. I only ate an <u>ice cream</u> during the game.

Helen: You must be both hungry. Joe can order something online for you.

Mom: Is there anything to eat in the kitchen?

Helen: There are some <u>doughnuts</u>. However, there are only three left.

Dad: That's not enough. I'll quickly cook up some <u>pancakes</u> for us.

Answer the questions

1. Did their basketball team win?

2. What did Mom eat at the basketball game?

3. How many doughnuts are there in the kitchen?

4. What will Mom and Dad eat?

Write the nouns

1. Mom and Dad's basketball _____ lost.

2. Dad ate some ice cream during the _____ .

3. There are some doughnuts in the _____ .

4. Dad will cook up some _____ for both of them.

Take the test

Write the answer next to the letter "A"

A: ___ 1. Helen did not order any ___.

a. french fries　　　　　　b. fried chicken　　　　　　c. chicken nuggets

A: ___ 2. ___ is Tom's favorite food.

a. Charlie's Chicken　　　　b. Mexican　　　　　　　　c. Tacos

A: ___ 3. Helen thinks the ___ are delicious.

a. burritos　　　　　　　　b. onion rings　　　　　　　c. tacos

A: ___ 4. Tom ordered some french fries with his burrito.

a. True.　　　　　　　　　b. False.　　　　　　　　　　c. Not given.

A: ___ 5. Did their basketball team win?

a. Yes.　　　　　　　　　b. No.　　　　　　　　　　　c. The score was even.

A: ___ 6. Mom ate a ___ during the game.

a. cheeseburger　　　　　b. taco　　　　　　　　　　c. hot dog

A: ___ 7. There are ___ doughnuts in the kitchen.

a. two　　　　　　　　　　b. three　　　　　　　　　　c. no

A: ___ 8. Which fast food was not mentioned?

a. Cheeseburger.　　　　　b. Burrito.　　　　　　　　　c. Pancake.

Answers on Page 206

Lesson 32: Landscapes

phong cảnh

Learn the words

1. mountain — núi
2. forest — rừng
3. beach — biển
4. river — sông
5. volcano — núi lửa
6. island — đảo
7. jungle — rừng nhiệt đới
8. waterfall — thác nước
9. lake — hồ
10. ocean — đại dương

Q&A Pattern 1

Which <u>island</u> are we staying at?
We're staying at the one which has a <u>volcano</u>.

Q&A Pattern 2

Is the hotel near the <u>ocean</u>?
Yes, it is.

Q&A Pattern 3

Can we visit some of the <u>lakes</u> while we're there?
Yes, of course we can.

Conversation 1

Dad: Stan, your mother and I have a surprise for you.

Stan: You do? What's the surprise?

Mom: We're going to take a trip to Hawaii this summer.

Dad: We know it's your dream to go surfing at a <u>beach</u> there.

Stan: It is! Which <u>island</u> are we staying at?

Dad: We're staying at the one that has a <u>volcano</u>.

Mom: I look forward to go hiking in the <u>mountains</u>.

Dad: They are very special. It will be nice to walk through tropical <u>forests</u>.

Stan: I'm so excited! When are we going there?

Dad: First, we have to book a hotel. I have to do that today.

Answer the questions

1. At which island in Hawaii will they be staying?

2. What is Stan's dream?

3. What does Mom look forward to doing?

4. What does Dad have to do today?

Complete the sentences using three words

1. They are going to take a trip to _____.

2. They are staying at the island that _____.

3. Mom looks forward to hiking _____.

4. Dad first has to _____.

Conversation 2

Dad: I was able to book a hotel in Hawaii for the first week of summer.

Stan: How many days will we be staying there?

Dad: We'll be staying there for eight days.

Stan: Is the hotel near the <u>ocean</u>?

Dad: Yes, it is. We can view it from our hotel room.

Mom: There's a clean <u>river</u> nearby that people can swim in.

Dad: The person at the hotel said there's a <u>waterfall</u> that we can visit.

Stan: Can we visit some of the <u>lakes</u> while we're there?

Mom: Yes, of course we can. Some of them are very beautiful.

Dad: That sounds like a great day for a picnic.

Answer the questions

1. How many days will they be staying in Hawaii?

2. What can they see from the hotel?

3. What did the person at the hotel tell Dad?

4. What does Dad want to do when they go to the lake?

Which person?

1. _____ booked a hotel in Hawaii.

2. _____ wants to know if the hotel is near the ocean.

3. _____ wants to visit the lakes in Hawaii.

4. _____ thinks some of the lakes are very beautiful.

Take the test

Write the answer next to the letter "A"

A: ___ **1.** Stan's dream is to go ___ in Hawaii.

a. hiking   b. diving   c. surfing

A: ___ **2.** Mom is looking forward ___ hiking in the mountains.

a. for   b. to   c. of

A: ___ **3.** "It will be ___ to walk through tropical forests."

a. clean   b. nice   c. excited

A: ___ **4.** ___ will book the hotel.

a. Mom   b. Stan   c. Dad

A: ___ **5.** They will go to Hawaii in the ___ week of summer.

a. first   b. second   c. third

A: ___ **6.** The family will take an airplane to Hawaii and stay for eight days.

a. True.   b. False.   c. Not given.

A: ___ **7.** You can see the ___ from the hotel room.

a. lake   b. ocean   c. waterfall

A: ___ **8.** Dad wants to have a picnic at the ___.

a. beach   b. river   c. lake

Answers on Page 206

Lesson 33: Homework

bài tập về nhà

Learn the words

1. **workbook** — sách bài tập
2. **vocabulary words** — từ vựng
3. **quiz** — đố
4. **science project** — dự án khoa học
5. **speech** — phát biểu
6. **article** — bài báo
7. **poster** — áp phích
8. **presentation** — trình bày
9. **essay** — tiểu luận
10. **report** — bài báo cáo

Q&A Pattern 1

Have you learned the <u>vocabulary words</u> yet?
No, I haven't.

Q&A Pattern 2

When is the <u>quiz</u> going to happen?
It's tomorrow.

Q&A Pattern 3

What else did you do for the <u>presentation</u>?
I made a <u>poster</u> as well.

Conversation 1

Lucy: Have you learned the vocabulary words yet?

Scott: No, I haven't. Are they difficult this week?

Lucy: Yes, they are much more difficult than last week's words.

Scott: There are activity sheets in the workbook to learn them.

Lucy: I finished those, but I still need to practice.

Scott: When is the quiz going to happen?

Lucy: It's tomorrow. You better start learning the words.

Scott: I have to make a speech tomorrow. I need to prepare for it.

Lucy: You have a lot of homework tonight.

Scott: Yes, I better stop talking with you on the phone and start!

Answer the questions

1. What does Lucy think about this week's vocabulary words?

2. Where are there activity sheets to learn the words?

3. What does Scott need to do tomorrow?

4. Who has a lot of homework tonight?

Put the sentences in order

The workbook has worksheets to learn the words. ___

Scott hasn't learned the vocabulary words yet. (1)

Scott has to prepare for his speech. ___

The quiz for the vocabulary words is tomorrow. ___

Conversation 2

Lucy: You look really tired. What time did you go to bed last night?

Scott: I was up until midnight preparing the speech for today's science class.

Lucy: I'm happy that I've already finished mine.

Scott: Yours was very well done. That's why I prepared more for mine.

Lucy: What else did you do for the presentation?

Scott: I made a poster as well. This took a while to finish.

Lucy: I'm sure you'll get a good grade for this science project.

Scott: I hope so. I've never done well in science.

Lucy: First, we have an English quiz. Did you get a chance to learn the words?

Scott: I looked over the vocabulary words, but I couldn't learn them all.

Answer the questions

1. What time did Scott go to sleep last night?
2. What does Scott think about Lucy's science presentation?
3. What did Scott make for the presentation?
4. In which class do they have a quiz?

Noun, Verb or Adjective?

chance ☐ Noun ☐ Verb ☐ ADJ   **words** ☐ Noun ☐ Verb ☐ ADJ

tired ☐ Noun ☐ Verb ☐ ADJ   **happy** ☐ Noun ☐ Verb ☐ ADJ

finish ☐ Noun ☐ Verb ☐ ADJ   **done** ☐ Noun ☐ Verb ☐ ADJ

grade ☐ Noun ☐ Verb ☐ ADJ   **made** ☐ Noun ☐ Verb ☐ ADJ

Take the test

Write the answer next to the letter "A"

A: ___ **1.** Scott hasn't ___ the vocabulary words yet.

a. learn   b. learns   c. learned

A: ___ **2.** There ___ activity sheets in the workbook.

a. have   b. are   c. is

A: ___ **3.** "I finished those, ___ I still need to practice."

a. so   b. but   c. because

A: ___ **4.** Scott needs to prepare for tomorrow's ___.

a. speech   b. article   c. report

A: ___ **5.** Lucy thinks Scott looks really ___.

a. tired   b. happy   c. good

A: ___ **6.** It took Scott a while to finish the ___.

a. workbook   b. poster   c. essay

A: ___ **7.** Lucy is ___ Scott will get a good grade for his science project.

a. think   b. sure   c. believe

A: ___ **8.** Scott didn't learn four of the words for the English quiz.

a. True.   b. False.   c. Not given.

Answers on Page 206

Lesson 34: The calendar

lịch

Learn the words

1. **class** — lớp học
2. **birthday** — sinh nhật
3. **party** — buổi tiệc
4. **competition** — cuộc thi
5. **speech** — phát biểu
6. **test** — kiểm tra
7. **meeting** — cuộc gặp
8. **recital** — buổi trình diễn
9. **appointment** — cuộc hẹn
10. **day off** — ngày nghỉ

Q&A Pattern 1

Do we have any <u>tests</u> on Monday?
No, we don't.

Q&A Pattern 2

How about we go out for dinner on Thursday?
I have a doctor's <u>appointment</u> on that day.

Q&A Pattern 3

Are you busy on Friday?
Yes, I have a <u>meeting</u>.

Conversation 1

Lucy: Your speech in science class today was very good!

Scott: Thank you. I worked really hard on it.

Lucy: You need a day off. We should do something fun this weekend.

Scott: I agree. Do we have any tests on Monday?

Lucy: No, we don't. Let's meet on Sunday.

Scott: I have a tennis competition in the morning. I can meet you after that.

Lucy: Great! I'm writing it down in my calendar now.

Scott: I have one, but I forget to write things in it.

Lucy: If I didn't use a calendar, I would be very disorganized.

Scott: I am disorganized now! Maybe I should start using mine!

Answer the questions

1. Why does Lucy think Scott needs a day off?

2. Are there any tests on Monday?

3. When is Scott's tennis competition?

4. What does Scott forget to do?

Unscramble the words

1. class / very / in / good / Scott's / was / speech / science

2. do / wants / weekend / Lucy / this / fun / something / to

3. in / morning / a / the / competition / Scott / tennis / has

4. his / using / calendar / should / Scott / start

Conversation 2

Mom: It's your <u>birthday</u> next Wednesday. What should we do?

Lucy: I have a <u>recital</u> on Thursday, so I need to practice on Wednesday night.

Mom: How about we go out for dinner on Thursday?

Dad: I have a doctor's <u>appointment</u> on that day.

Mom: We may have to celebrate on Saturday.

Lucy: Are you busy on Friday?

Mom: Yes, I have a <u>meeting</u>. I won't be back until later.

Dad: Your mother and I are both free on Saturday.

Lucy: I only have a piano <u>class</u> at two o'clock.

Mom: Great! I'll book a table at the restaurant now.

Answer the questions

1. What does Lucy need to practice for?

2. When is Dad's doctor's appointment?

3. When will they celebrate Lucy's birthday?

4. What time is Lucy's piano class?

Find three nouns, verbs and adjectives

Nouns	Verbs	Adjectives
1. _____	1. _____	2. _____
2. _____	2. _____	2. _____
3. _____	3. _____	3. _____

Take the test

Write the answer next to the letter "A"

A: ___ **1.** Lucy wants to meet Scott on ___.

a. Thursday	b. Sunday	c. Monday

A: ___ **2.** Scott has a tennis ___ in the morning.

a. class	b. test	c. competition

A: ___ **3.** "If I didn't use a calendar, I __ be very disorganized."

a. will	b. would	c. do

A: ___ **4.** Scott should ___ using a calendar.

a. start	b. starts	c. starting

A: ___ **5.** Whose birthday is it next week?

a. It's Scott's birthday.	b. It's Dad's birthday.	c. It's Lucy's birthday.

A: ___ **6.** Lucy has a ___ on Thursday.

a. speech	b. recital	c. piano class

A: ___ **7.** Mom has a meeting on Friday, so she can't go out for dinner on that day.

a. True.	b. False.	c. Not given.

A: ___ **8.** The family will celebrate Lucy's birthday on ___.

a. Friday	b. Saturday	c. Sunday

Answers on Page 206

Lesson 35 — Camping

cắm trại

Learn the words

1. a barbecue
   nướng ngoài trời
2. a gas bottle
   la bàn
3. sleeping bags
   túi ngủ
4. plastic dishes
   đĩa nhựa
5. fishing rods
   cần câu
6. binoculars
   ống nhòm
7. a flashlight
   đèn pin
8. a tent
   lều
9. a compass
   la bàn
10. a cooler
    cắm trại hộp mát

Q&A Pattern 1

How do you cook food?
We usually have a <u>barbecue</u>.

Q&A Pattern 2

How do you keep the food cold?
We keep the food and drinks on ice in the <u>cooler</u>.

Q&A Pattern 3

What do you want me to pack first?
You can pack the <u>fishing rods</u> first.

Conversation 1

Scott: I can't meet you this Sunday. My parents want to take me camping.

Lucy: That's fine. We'll get together another time. Where will you be going?

Scott: There's a river where we like to put up a <u>tent</u> next to.

Lucy: I've never been camping. How do you cook food?

Scott: We usually have a <u>barbecue</u>. It's a lot of fun.

Lucy: I've never cooked food outside. Do you prepare a fire?

Scott: No, we don't. We bring a <u>gas bottle</u>.

Lucy: I see. How do you keep the food and drinks cold?

Scott: We keep the food and drinks on ice in the <u>cooler</u>.

Lucy: Wow. You really know how to go camping.

Answer the questions

1. Why can't Scott meet Lucy on Sunday?
2. Where do Scott's family go camping?
3. Will they use fire to cook the food?
4. Where do they put the food and drinks to keep them cool?

Fill in the blanks

Lucy: I've _____ been _____. How _____ you _____ food?

Scott: We _____ have a _____. It's a _____ of _____.

Lucy: I've never _____ food _____. Do you _____ a _____?

Scott: No, we _____. We _____ a _____ bottle.

Conversation 2

Dad: Can you help me put things in the car for the camping trip?

Scott: Sure. What do you want me to pack first?

Dad: You can pack the <u>fishing rods</u> first.

Scott: Are you sure we need them? Last time, we didn't catch a fish!

Dad: Of course, we will! We're going to fill up the <u>cooler</u> with fish.

Mom: Ha! We should bring some extra food just in case.

Scott: Do you know where the <u>flashlight</u> is?

Mom: It's in the top drawer in the kitchen. The <u>plastic dishes</u> are there, too.

Dad: Have you packed the <u>sleeping bags</u> yet?

Mom: Yes, they've already been put in the car.

Answer the questions

1. What does Dad want Scott to help him do?

2. Why does Scott ask Dad if they need to bring fishing rods?

3. Where is the flashlight?

4. What is already in the car?

Past, Present or Future?

1. Last time, we didn't catch a fish! ☐ **Past** ☐ **Present** ☐ **Future**

2. We're going to fill up the cooler with fish. ☐ **Past** ☐ **Present** ☐ **Future**

3. We should bring some extra food just in case. ☐ **Past** ☐ **Present** ☐ **Future**

4. It's in the top drawer in the kitchen. ☐ **Past** ☐ **Present** ☐ **Future**

Take the test

Write the answer next to the letter "A"

A: ___ **1.** Scott's family likes to put up a tent by the ___.

a. river   b. lake   c. ocean

A: ___ **2.** Lucy has ___ been camping before.

a. ever   b. neither   c. never

A: ___ **3.** They prepare a ___ to cook the food.

a. fire   b. stove   c. gas bottle

A: ___ **4.** Scott's family uses a cooler to keep the food and drinks cold.

a. True.   b. False.   c. Not given.

A: ___ **5.** Dad told Scott to pack the ___ first.

a. sleeping bags   b. fishing rods   c. plastic dishes

A: ___ **6.** Scott is unsure they need fishing rods because they ___.

a. will have a barbecue   b. didn't catch a fish last time   c. have food in the cooler

A: ___ **7.** The flashlight is in the ___ drawer in the kitchen.

a. bottom   b. middle   c. top

A: ___ **8.** The ___ have already been put in the car.

a. plastic dishes   b. sleeping bags   c. gas bottle

Answers on Page 206

Lesson 36: Daily life

cuộc sống hàng ngày

Learn the words

1. **woken up**
   thức dậy
2. **brushed my teeth**
   đánh răng
3. **done homework**
   làm xong bài tập về nhà
4. **taken out the trash**
   vứt rác
5. **cooked dinner**
   nấu bữa tối
6. **eaten breakfast**
   ăn sáng
7. **gone to school**
   đi học
8. **taken a shower**
   tắm
9. **gone shopping**
   đi mua sắm
10. **gone to sleep**
    đã đi ngủ

Q&A Pattern 1

Are you ready to celebrate your birthday?
Almost. I haven't <u>taken a shower</u> yet.

Q&A Pattern 2

Have you already <u>cooked dinner</u>?
No, I haven't.

Q&A Pattern 3

Would you like to <u>eat breakfast</u> together?
Yes, I would like that very much.

Conversation 1

Dad: Are you ready to celebrate your birthday?

Lucy: Almost. I haven't <u>taken a shower</u> yet.

Dad: Have you already <u>cooked dinner</u>?

Mom: No, I haven't. We're going to Lucy's favorite restaurant.

Dad: Great. I love Chinese food and I'm also really hungry!

Mom: That's because you didn't <u>eat breakfast</u> this morning.

Dad: Yes, and I only ate a salad for lunch.

Lucy: What time do you think we'll be home? I haven't <u>done</u> any <u>homework</u>.

Mom: It's your birthday. Do it tomorrow. Now, let's go out!

Dad: As soon as I've <u>taken out the trash</u>, we can leave.

Answer the questions

1. Where are they going to celebrate Lucy's birthday?
2. Why is Dad very hungry?
3. Has Lucy done her homework yet?
4. What does Dad want to do before they leave?

True or False?

1. Lucy has not taken a shower yet.   ☐ True ☐ False
2. Mom decided to cook Lucy's favorite food.   ☐ True ☐ False
3. Dad didn't eat breakfast this morning.   ☐ True ☐ False
4. They will go to a Chinese restaurant for dinner.   ☐ True ☐ False

Conversation 2

Lucy: It's nice to be with you both. Thanks for taking me to this restaurant.

Mom: The family should get together more often.

Dad: I agree, but our daily lives are so busy.

Lucy: That's true. By the time I <u>wake up</u>, you've already gone to work.

Mom: We were both home last night, but I didn't see you at all.

Lucy: That's because I was <u>doing homework</u> in my bedroom.

Dad: And I was busy in the kitchen <u>cooking dinner</u>.

Mom: Would you like to <u>eat breakfast</u> together?

Lucy: Yes, I would like that very much. We can do that before I <u>go to school</u>.

Mom: Now, what do you want to order for dinner?

Answer the questions

1. Where are they now?

2. Where was Lucy doing her homework last night?

3. What was Dad doing last night?

4. What does Mom want to do in the morning with Lucy?

Write the verbs

1. Lucy thanked her parents for _____ her to the restaurant.

2. Lucy was _____ homework in her bedroom.

3. Dad was busy in the kitchen _____ dinner.

4. Mom wants to _____ breakfast with Lucy.

Take the test

Write the answer next to the letter "A"

A: ___ **1.** Lucy needed to ___.

a. take a shower	b. cook dinner	c. brush her teeth

A: ___ **2.** Mom decided not to ___.

a. cook dinner	b. do homework	c. take a shower

A: ___ **3.** Who didn't eat breakfast this morning?

a. Mom.	b. Dad.	c. Lucy.

A: ___ **4.** What did Mom tell Lucy to do tomorrow?

a. Take out the trash.	b. Cook dinner.	c. Her homework.

A: ___ **5.** By the time Lucy wakes up, Dad has already ___.

a. eaten breakfast	b. gone to work	c. brushed his teeth

A: ___ **6.** Mom didn't see Lucy last night because she was doing homework.

a. True.	b. False.	c. Not given.

A: ___ **7.** Who cooked dinner last night?

a. Mom.	b. Lucy.	c. Dad.

A: ___ **8.** Mom and Lucy want to ___ together tomorrow.

a. eat breakfast	b. go shopping	c. go to school

Answers on Page 206

Lesson 37 — On the street

trên đường

Learn the words

1. a bus
   một chiếc xe buýt
2. a truck
   xe tải
3. an ambulance
   xe cứu thương
4. a fire engine
   một động cơ cứu hỏa
5. some traffic lights
   một số đèn giao thông
6. a fire hydrant
   một vòi cứu hỏa
7. a stop sign
   bảng hiệu dừng lại
8. a trash can
   một thùng rác
9. some shops
   vài cửa hàng
10. a police car
    một chiếc xe cảnh sát

Q&A Pattern 1

Which siren is that?
It's a <u>fire engine</u> siren.

Q&A Pattern 2

Does that mean we can't get to the <u>shops</u> by car?
Yes, it does.

Q&A Pattern 3

Could they be putting up new <u>traffic lights</u>?
Yes, they could be.

Conversation 1

Ross: I can hear something in the background. Which siren is that?

Bill: It's a fire engine siren. There was a car accident at the corner of the street.

Ross: I hope nobody got hurt. Is there a fire?

Bill: There's no fire. A car tried to avoid a truck and hit a fire hydrant.

Ross: I guess the firefighters have gone down to fix it.

Bill: I think so. I didn't see an ambulance go there, so nobody got hurt.

Ross: How often does this happen?

Bill: It happens quite often. They need to put traffic lights at the corner.

Ross: It's different here in the country. We seldom have car accidents.

Bill: Living in the city is great, but you have to be careful on the street.

Answer the questions

1. What were the firefighters doing?

2. Why does Bill think nobody got hurt?

3. What does Bill think they should put at the corner?

4. Are there many car accidents in the country?

Complete the sentences using three words

1. Ross can hear something _____ _____ .

2. The car hit _____ _____ .

3. There was no ambulance, so _____ _____ .

4. Bill thinks they should put traffic lights _____ _____ .

Conversation 2

Bill: Why is there a police car in front of our building?

Nancy: I think they are closing the end of the street to fix the corner.

Bill: Does that mean we can't get to the shops by car?

Nancy: Yes, it does. The buses aren't running either.

Bill: I wonder what they're still fixing.

Nancy: The fire hydrant was knocked over in the accident.

Bill: The firefighters already fixed it yesterday.

Nancy: I saw the roadworkers removing the old stop sign.

Bill: Could they be putting up new traffic lights?

Nancy: Yes, they could be. That would make the corner much safer!

Answer the questions

1. What is in front of the building?
2. Can they get to the shops by car?
3. What happened to the fire hydrant?
4. What did Nancy see the roadworkers doing?

Which person?

1. _____ is wondering why the roadworkers are still working.
2. _____ said the firefighters already fixed the fire hydrant.
3. _____ saw roadworkers removing the old stop sign.
4. _____ thinks traffic lights would make the corner safer.

Take the test

Write the answer next to the letter "A"

A: ____ **1.** What kind of siren was in the background?

a. An ambulance.   b. A fire engine.   c. A police car.

A: ____ **2.** "A car tried to avoid a ____ and hit a ____."

a. truck, fire hydrant   b. bus, stop sign   c. police car, trash can

A: ____ **3.** Bill thinks nobody got hurt because he didn't see ____.

a. a fire   b. an ambulance   c. a police car

A: ____ **4.** "It's different here in the country. We ____ have car accidents."

a. often   b. seldom   c. never

A: ____ **5.** They can only get to the shops by walking there.

a. True.   b. False.   c. Not given.

A: ____ **6.** The roadworkers were ____ the old stop sign.

a. removed   b. remove   c. removing

A: ____ **7.** Putting up ____ would make the corner safer.

a. a stop sign   b. traffic lights   c. a fire hydrant

A: ____ **8.** What was not mentioned?

a. A bus.   b. The shops.   c. A trash can.

Answers on Page 206

Lesson 38: Hobbies

sở thích

Learn the words

1. **listen to music**
   nghe nhạc
2. **play video games**
   chơi trò chơi điện tử
3. **take photographs**
   chụp ảnh
4. **do some gardening**
   làm vườn
5. **go hiking**
   đi bộ đường dài
6. **sing karaoke**
   hát karaoke
7. **go fishing**
   đi câu cá
8. **watch movies**
   xem phim
9. **go camping**
   đi cắm trại
10. **play chess**
    chơi cờ

Q&A Pattern 1

What are you planning to do with your friend?
We're planning to <u>play video games</u>.

Q&A Pattern 2

Who taught you how to <u>play chess</u>?
The teacher taught us.

Q&A Pattern 3

What should we do outside?
We could <u>go fishing</u> at the lake.

Conversation 1

Dad: What are you planning to do with your friend?

Joe: We're planning to play video games.

Dad: Don't play all day. It's a great day to be outside.

Joe: We might go to the cinema to watch a movie.

Mom: That's still inside. It's a sunny day. You should do something outdoors.

Joe: Stan and I recently started playing chess. We could do that outside.

Dad: Who taught you how to play chess?

Joe: The teacher taught us. There's a chess club that Stan and I joined.

Mom: That's excellent! I didn't know there was a chess club at school.

Joe: It only started four weeks ago.

Answer the questions

1. How is the weather today?
2. What did Mom suggest Joe and his friend should do?
3. What have Joe and Stan started doing?
4. How long has the chess club been going for?

Put the sentences in order

Dad wants Joe to do something outside. ___

Mom didn't know there was a chess club at school. ___

Joe is planning to play video games with his friend. (1)

Stan and Joe have recently started playing chess. ___

Conversation 2

Joe: My parents think we should do something outside today.

Stan: I don't mind. What should we do outside?

Joe: We could go fishing at the lake.

Stan: I don't want to. I did that when I went camping last weekend.

Joe: Did you catch any big fish?

Stan: No, we didn't. The fish in the river weren't very hungry that day.

Joe: I'm not sure what to do today. Hey, Helen. What are you doing today?

Helen: I'm meeting a few friends from school later to sing karaoke.

Stan: That sounds like fun. I've never done that before.

Helen: You can join us. I'm listening to music now to learn the songs.

Answer the questions

1. When did Stan go fishing?
2. Why did Stan think he didn't catch any fish?
3. Which friends will Helen be meeting later?
4. Why is Helen listening to music?

Noun, Verb or Adjective?

join ☐ Noun ☐ Verb ☐ ADJ   **fun** ☐ Noun ☐ Verb ☐ ADJ

big ☐ Noun ☐ Verb ☐ ADJ   **catch** ☐ Noun ☐ Verb ☐ ADJ

parents ☐ Noun ☐ Verb ☐ ADJ   **hungry** ☐ Noun ☐ Verb ☐ ADJ

river ☐ Noun ☐ Verb ☐ ADJ   **friends** ☐ Noun ☐ Verb ☐ ADJ

Take the test

Write the answer next to the letter "A"

A: ___ **1.** Joe is planning to play video games with Dad.

a. True.	b. False.	c. Not given.

A: ___ **2.** Mom wants Joe to do something ___.

a. inside	b. outside	c. at school

A: ___ **3.** Stan and Joe recently ___ playing chess.

a. start	b. starting	c. started

A: ___ **4.** The chess club started four ___ ago.

a. days	b. weeks	c. months

A: ___ **5.** Stan doesn't want to go ___.

a. hiking	b. fishing	c. camping

A: ___ **6.** "The fish in the river ___ very hungry that day."

a. weren't	b. aren't	c. didn't

A: ___ **7.** Stan has never ___.

a. gone hiking	b. watched movies	c. sung karaoke

A: ___ **8.** Helen is listening to music ___.

a. to learn the songs	b. to relax	c. for fun

Answers on Page 206

Lesson 39: In the bedroom

trong phòng ngủ

Learn the words

1. **pillow**
   cái gối
2. **bed**
   giường
3. **blanket**
   cái mền
4. **drawers**
   ngăn kéo
5. **mattress**
   nệm
6. **alarm clock**
   đồng hồ báo thức
7. **lamp**
   đèn
8. **bed sheets**
   ga trải giường
9. **nightstand**
   đầu giường
10. **wardrobe**
    tủ quần áo

Q&A Pattern 1

What do you need for your bedroom?
I need a new wardrobe.

Q&A Pattern 2

What do you think about this wardrobe?
I like the color of it.

Q&A Pattern 3

How much does everything cost?
The wardrobe and drawers cost five hundred dollars.

Conversation 1

Pam: Now that I've finished the living room, I can start on my bedroom.

Fran: What do you need for your bedroom?

Pam: I need a new <u>wardrobe</u>. The one I have now is much too old.

Fran: What's wrong with it?

Pam: The doors don't close properly. It's very annoying.

Fran: I would love to get a new <u>mattress</u> for my <u>bed</u>.

Pam: You should come with me to the furniture store.

Fran: I would love to. A reading <u>lamp</u> would be nice, too.

Pam: Let's go tomorrow morning. I'll pick you up at eight o'clock.

Fran: That sounds good. I'll set my <u>alarm clock</u> now.

Answer the questions

1. What does Pam need for her bedroom?

2. What's wrong with Pam's wardrobe?

3. What does Fran want to get?

4. What time will Pam pick up Fran?

Unscramble the words

1. new / wardrobe / a / Pam / needs

2. close / doors / properly / The / don't

3. to / a / mattress / Fran / get / would / new / love

4. up / o'clock / at / Pam / eight / pick / Fran / will

Conversation 2

Fran: What do you think about this <u>wardrobe</u>?

Pam: I like the color of it. It would look perfect in my bedroom.

Fran: It comes with these <u>drawers</u> as well.

Pam: That's great. How much does everything cost?

Fran: The <u>wardrobe</u> and <u>drawers</u> cost five hundred dollars.

Pam: That's a little expensive, but I really want them in my bedroom!

Fran: I think you should get them. Now, let's get a <u>mattress</u> for me.

Pam: Yes, let's do that. Hey, look at these <u>pillows</u>.

Fran: They would look good on my <u>bed</u>. I want to get one.

Pam: Here are some matching <u>bed sheets</u>. You must get them, too!

Answer the questions

1. What does Pam think about the color of the wardrobe?

2. How much do the wardrobe and drawers cost?

3. What does Pam think about the price?

4. Does Fran want to get a pillow?

Find three nouns, verbs and adjectives

Nouns

1. _____

2. _____

3. _____

Verbs

1. _____

2. _____

3. _____

Adjectives

2. _____

2. _____

3. _____

Take the test

Write the answer next to the letter "A"

A: ___ **1.** Pam has finished the ___.

a. bedroom	b. bathroom	c. living room

A: ___ **2.** The wardrobe Pam has now is ___ and the doors don't close properly.

a. too small	b. too old	c. broken

A: ___ **3.** Fran wants to get a ___ for her bedroom.

a. wardrobe	b. nightstand	c. mattress

A: ___ **4.** The girls will go to the furniture store in the ___.

a. morning	b. afternoon	c. evening

A: ___ **5.** What does Pam like about the wardrobe at the furniture store?

a. The size.	b. The color.	c. The drawers.

A: ___ **6.** The wardrobe and drawers cost ___ hundred dollars.

a. five	b. four	c. three

A: ___ **7.** The pillow comes with ___ bed sheets.

a. matching	b. matched	c. match

A: ___ **8.** Which bedroom item was not mentioned?

a. A lamp.	b. A blanket.	c. An alarm clock.

Answers on Page 206

Lesson 40: More places

thêm địa điểm

Learn the words

1. school — trường học
2. library — thư viện
3. police station — cảnh sát
4. hospital — bệnh viện
5. train station — nhà ga
6. factory — nhà máy
7. office — văn phòng
8. fire station — trạm cứu hỏa
9. clinic — trạm y tế
10. bus stop — điểm dừng xe buýt

Q&A Pattern 1

What do you think about moving closer to the <u>school</u>?
I think it's a good idea.

Q&A Pattern 2

Isn't there a <u>hospital</u> on that street?
Yes, that's right.

Q&A Pattern 3

Do you have another house?
I have one across from the <u>train station</u>.

Conversation 1

Mom: It would be great to live closer to town.

Dad: I'd rather move to a place that's near my <u>office</u>.

Mom: No, there's a <u>factory</u> near there. The air is too polluted in that area.

Helen: That's true. I don't like catching a bus to <u>school</u> every day.

Joe: Neither do I. Standing at the <u>bus stop</u> in winter is terrible.

Helen: I agree. It's freezing in the mornings.

Mom: What do you think about moving closer to the <u>school</u>?

Dad: I think it's a good idea.

Helen: There's also a <u>library</u> nearby. Joe and I could study there.

Mom: I'll see if there are any houses available in that area.

Answer the questions

1. Why doesn't Mom want to live near the office?

2. What doesn't Helen like doing?

3. What does Dad think about moving closer to the school?

4. What is near the school? _____

Fill in the blanks

Mom: It _____ be _____ to live _____ to town.

Dad: I'd _____ move to a _____ that's near my _____.

Mom: No, there's a _____ near _____. The air is too _____ in that _____.

Helen: That's _____. I _____ like _____ a bus to _____ every day.

Conversation 2

Mom: Are there any houses near the school?

Steve: There are a few. I'm selling one on Dove Street.

Mom: Isn't there a <u>hospital</u> on that street?

Steve: Yes, that's right. The <u>fire station</u> is around the corner as well.

Mom: I'm concerned it could be quite noisy there.

Steve: That's true. A lot of ambulances drive on that street.

Mom: I'd like to live in a quieter area. Do you have another house?

Steve: I have one across from the <u>train station</u>. The trains will also be noisy.

Mom: I wouldn't like to live there. I may have to wait for something better.

Steve: I'll contact you as soon as a new house comes available.

Answer the questions

1. On which street is there a hospital?
2. Why doesn't Mom want to live on Dove Street?
3. Where is the train station?
4. Where would Mom prefer to live?

Present or Future?

1. The fire station is around the corner as well.   ☐ **Present** ☐ **Future**
2. I'm concerned it could be quite noisy there.   ☐ **Present** ☐ **Future**
3. A lot of ambulances drive on that street.   ☐ **Present** ☐ **Future**
4. The trains will also be noisy.   ☐ **Present** ☐ **Future**

Take the test

Write the answer next to the letter "A"

A: ___ **1.** Mom would like to live ___ to town.

a. close   b. closer   c. closest

A: ___ **2.** "I'd ___ move to a place that's near my office."

a. rather than   b. prefer   c. rather

A: ___ **3.** Helen doesn't like ___.

a. air pollution   b. catching a bus to school c. the factory

A: ___ **4.** Joe thinks standing at the bus stop in winter is ___.

a. terrible   b. freezing   c. noisy

A: ___ **5.** The ___ is on Dove street.

a. fire station   b. train station   c. hospital

A: ___ **6.** Mom would like to live in a ___ area.

a. closer   b. quieter   c. better

A: ___ **7.** Steve is selling a house that is across from the ___ station.

a. train   b. police   c. fire

A: ___ **8.** There is a library near the school where Helen and Joe could study at.

a. True.   b. False.   c. Not given.

Answers on Page 206

Lesson 41: The face

khuôn mặt

Learn the words

1. **chin**
   cằm
2. **nose**
   mũi
3. **eye**
   mắt
4. **eyebrow**
   lông mày
5. **eyelash**
   lông mi
6. **ear**
   tai
7. **hair**
   tóc
8. **cheek**
   má
9. **mouth**
   miệng
10. **lip**
    môi

Q&A Pattern 1

How did your mother do her makeup?
My mother liked to put pink lipstick on her <u>lips</u>.

Q&A Pattern 2

Why don't you put makeup around your <u>eyes</u> now?
I don't have time to do that.

Q&A Pattern 3

Weren't your <u>ears</u> uncomfortable?
Yes, they were.

Conversation 1

Jill: Is this a photo of your mother?

Molly: Yes, it is. She was our age in that photo.

Jill: I love her <u>hair</u>. The style is really special.

Molly: I know. She used to have big <u>eyelashes</u>, too.

Jill: She was very pretty when she was younger.

Molly: Do you have any photos of your mother when she was younger?

Jill: Yes, I have a few. She looked very different.

Molly: How did your mother do her makeup?

Jill: My mother liked to put pink lipstick on her <u>lips</u>. She never does that now.

Molly: It's interesting how people change.

Answer the questions

1. What did Jill think of Molly's mother's hair?

2. Was Molly's mother pretty when she was younger?

3. What doesn't Jill's mother do now?

4. What does Molly think is interesting?

True or False?

1. They are looking at a photograph of Molly's mother. ☐ **True** ☐ **False**

2. Molly's mother does not have big eyelashes now. ☐ **True** ☐ **False**

3. Jill does not have any photographs of her mother. ☐ **True** ☐ **False**

4. Jill's mother never used to wear pink lipstick. ☐ **True** ☐ **False**

Conversation 2

Molly: Jill and I were looking at photos of you when you were younger.

Mom: Things were very different at that time.

Molly: Your <u>eyes</u> were very beautiful.

Mom: Girls used to like to have thin <u>eyebrows</u>.

Molly: I noticed that. Why don't you put makeup around your <u>eyes</u> now?

Mom: I don't have time to do that. Putting on <u>eyelashes</u> takes a lot of effort.

Molly: I also noticed that you used to wear large earrings on your <u>ears</u>.

Mom: That's true. They were very heavy!

Molly: Weren't your <u>ears</u> uncomfortable?

Mom: Yes, they were. I would never wear them now.

Answer the questions

1. What does Molly think about her mother's eyes?

2. How did girls used to have their eyebrows?

3. Why doesn't Mom put eyelashes on?

4. Why doesn't Mom never wear large earrings now?

Write the adjectives

1. Molly and Jill were looking at a photograph of Mom when she was _____.

2. Mom's eyes were _____.

3. The earrings were very _____.

4. Mom's ears were _____ when she wore the earrings.

Take the test

Write the answer next to the letter "A"

A: ___ **1.** The girls are looking at a photograph of ___.

a. Molly   b. Molly's mother   c. Molly's aunt

A: ___ **2.** Molly's mother is fifteen years old in the photograph.

a. True.   b. False.   c. Not given.

A: ___ **3.** Molly's mother used to have big ___.

a. eyebrows   b. eyes   c. eyelashes

A: ___ **4.** Who liked to put pink lipstick on?

a. Molly's mother.   b. Jill's mother.   c. Jilly and Molly.

A: ___ **5.** "Girls used to like to have ___ eyebrows."

a. thick   b. thin   c. big

A: ___ **6.** Mom doesn't put makeup around her eyes because she doesn't have ___.

a. time   b. makeup   c. effort

A: ___ **7.** Mom thinks ___ takes a lot of effort to put on eyelashes.

a. they   b. she   c. it

A: ___ **8.** Mom ___ never wear heavy earrings now.

a. would   b. could   c. should

Answers on Page 206

Lesson 42: Personalities

tính cách

Learn the words

1. shy
   nhút nhát
2. lazy
   lười biếng
3. outgoing
   hướng ngoại
4. generous
   hào phóng
5. studious
   ham học
6. interesting
   hấp dẫn
7. serious
   nghiêm trọng
8. funny
   buồn cười
9. smart
   thông minh
10. easygoing
    dễ tính

Q&A Pattern 1

What do you think of her?
She was very <u>serious</u>.

Q&A Pattern 2

Do you think Mr. Moody was <u>funny</u> today?
Yes, I do.

Q&A Pattern 3

What do you think about our new classmate?
He seems very <u>outgoing</u>.

Conversation 1

Stan: I had music class with the new teacher yesterday.

Abby: What do you think of her?

Stan: She was very <u>serious</u>. I thought you said she was friendly.

Abby: I did. When I spoke to her, she seemed really <u>easygoing</u>.

Stan: I think she expects everyone to be more <u>studious</u> in her class.

Abby: You should be fine. You're a very good musician.

Stan: I'm worried about having to perform in front of people in music class.

Abby: You shouldn't be so <u>shy</u>. I wish I could play music like you.

Stan: You could. You just need to practice more.

Abby: The truth is I'm a little <u>lazy</u> when it comes to learning music.

Answer the questions

1. Which class did Stan have yesterday?
2. What does Stan think about the music teacher?
3. What is Stan worried about doing?
4. Why can't Abby learn music well?

Complete the sentences using three words

1. Stan thinks the music teacher _____ .
2. The music teacher expects the students to _____ .
3. Abby thinks Stan is a _____ .
4. Stan thinks Abby needs _____ .

Conversation 2

Abby: Do you think Mr. Moody was <u>funny</u> today?

Stan: Yes, I do. He knows how to make math more <u>interesting</u>.

Abby: Did you find someone to help you?

Stan: My father said he can teach me. He is very <u>smart</u>.

Abby: I hope he can. I'm happy to help you if you need it.

Stan: That's very <u>generous</u> of you. I will study math harder this year.

Abby: You'll be fine if you be more <u>studious</u>.

Stan: What do you think about our new classmate?

Abby: He seems very <u>outgoing</u>. I saw Brian talking with a lot of people today.

Stan: That's true. He has already made a lot of friends.

Answer the questions

1. How was Mr. Moody in math class today?

2. Who is going to help Stan with his math?

3. What does Stan want to do this year?

4. Why does Abby think their new classmate is outgoing?

Which person?

1. _____ thinks Mr. Moody is funny.

2. _____ is happy to help Stan with math.

3. _____ thinks his father is very smart.

4. _____ has already made a lot of friends.

Take the test

Write the answer next to the letter "A"

A: ___ **1.** Stan had a ___ class yesterday with the new teacher.

a. music   b. math   c. history

A: ___ **2.** ___ thought the music teacher was serious.

a. Stan   b. Abby   c. Stan and Abby

A: ___ **3.** What does the music teacher expect the students to be?

a. Serious.   b. Studious.   c. Generous.

A: ___ **4.** "I'm worried about ___ to perform in front of people in music class."

a. have   b. had   c. having

A: ___ **5.** Mr. Moody knows how to make math more ___.

a. funny   b. easygoing   c. interesting

A: ___ **6.** Stan's father is very ___.

a. funny   b. smart   c. serious

A: ___ **7.** Abby thinks their new classmate is ___.

a. outgoing   b. easygoing   c. funny

A: ___ **8.** Their new classmate has already ___ a lot of friends.

a. get   b. made   c. had

Answers on Page 206

Lesson 43: Music

âm nhạc

Learn the words

1. **beautifully** — hay
2. **quietly** — khẽ khàng
3. **slowly** — chậm
4. **gracefully** — duyên dáng
5. **well** — tốt
6. **loudly** — lớn tiếng
7. **quickly** — nhanh
8. **terribly** — kinh khủng
9. **correctly** — đúng
10. **badly** — tệ

Q&A Pattern 1

How good are you at violin?
I play violin <u>badly</u>!

Q&A Pattern 2

Why do you need my help?
I want to play the song <u>beautifully</u>.

Q&A Pattern 3

Can you finish your homework <u>quickly</u>?
No, I can't.

Conversation 1

Abby: The teacher has asked me to perform in front of tomorrow's class.

Stan: How good are you at violin?

Abby: I play violin <u>badly</u>! I'm not as good as you.

Stan: I'm not that good. I just practice a lot.

Abby: You play the violin so <u>gracefully</u>. I can't even play it <u>correctly</u>!

Stan: When you get home, start learning the song <u>slowly</u>. You will improve.

Abby: I'm <u>terribly</u> nervous. I don't know what to do.

Stan: Calm down. Practice makes perfect.

Abby: I'll need to practice all night to play the song <u>well</u> by tomorrow.

Stan: Your brother, Joe, is a good musician. You can ask him for help.

Answer the questions

1. What does the teacher want Abby to do?

2. How does Abby think Stan plays the violin?

3. How is Abby feeling?

4. Who does Stan think is a good musician?

Put the sentences in order

Dad wants Joe to do something outside. ___

Mom didn't know there was a chess club at school. (1)

Joe is planning to play video games with his friend. ___

Stan and Joe have recently started playing chess. ___

Conversation 2

Abby: Joe, I need your help with learning this song.

Joe: Why do you need my help?

Abby: I want to play the song <u>beautifully</u>.

Joe: That's not going to be easy for you. You don't practice enough.

Abby: I know, but I need to play it <u>well</u> by tomorrow. It's hard for me.

Joe: I can help you after I finish my math homework.

Abby: Thanks, but hurry. Can you finish your homework <u>quickly</u>?

Joe: No, I can't. I have a lot of questions to do.

Abby: I'll start practicing in my bedroom while you do them.

Joe: Don't play too <u>loudly</u>. I need to concentrate on my homework.

Answer the questions

1. How does Abby want to play the song?

2. Why does Joe think it will be difficult for Abby to play the song beautifully?

3. Why can't Joe finish the math homework quickly?

4. Where will Abby start practicing?

Noun, Verb or Adjective?

homework ☐ Noun ☐ Verb ☐ ADJ

play ☐ Noun ☐ Verb ☐ ADJ

easy ☐ Noun ☐ Verb ☐ ADJ

concentrate ☐ Noun ☐ Verb ☐ ADJ

practice ☐ Noun ☐ Verb ☐ ADJ

hard ☐ Noun ☐ Verb ☐ ADJ

questions ☐ Noun ☐ Verb ☐ ADJ

bedroom ☐ Noun ☐ Verb ☐ ADJ

Take the test

Write the answer next to the letter "A"

A: ___ **1.** Abby thinks she plays the violin ___.

a. well   b. correctly   c. badly

A: ___ **2.** Abby thinks she doesn't play violin as well as Stan.

a. True.   b. False.   c. Not given.

A: ___ **3.** Abby is feeling ___ about tomorrow's performance.

a. calm   b. perfect   c. nervous

A: ___ **4.** "I'll need to practice ___ night to play the song well by tomorrow."

a. every   b. all   c. at

A: ___ **5.** Abby wants to play the song ___.

a. gracefully   b. correctly   c. beautifully

A: ___ **6.** Joe will help Abby ___ he finishes his homework.

a. before   b. after   c. while

A: ___ **7.** Abby ___ practicing in her bedroom.

a. will start   b. start   c. will be starting

A: ___ **8.** Joe doesn't want Abby to play ___.

a. slowly   b. quickly   c. loudly

Answers on Page 206

Lesson 44 — Activities

hoạt động

Learn the words

1. **play piano**
   chơi đàn piano
2. **read books**
   đọc sách
3. **play video games**
   chơi trò chơi điện tử
4. **surf the internet**
   lướt mạng
5. **take photographs**
   chụp ảnh
6. **watch TV**
   xem Ti vi
7. **sing songs**
   hát nhạc
8. **study English**
   học tiếng Anh
9. **play cards**
   chơi bài
10. **go shopping**
    đi mua sắm

Q&A Pattern 1

What have you been up to?
I've been <u>surfing the internet</u>.

Q&A Pattern 2

What should we do?
We could <u>play video games</u>.

Q&A Pattern 3

Who's that <u>playing piano</u> in the living room?
That's my cousin, Joe.

Conversation 1

Tom: Hello, it's Tom here. Is John there?

Mom: Hi, Tom. Yes, he's <u>watching TV</u>. I'll go and get him.

John: Hey, thanks for calling. What have you been up to?

Tom: I've been <u>surfing the internet</u> all morning. I'm pretty bored.

John: Me, too. I usually walk to the library to <u>read books</u>, but it's raining today.

Tom: We should get together and do something.

John: I'm about to <u>go shopping</u>, but you can come over when I get back.

Tom: That sounds good. What should we do?

John: We could <u>play video games</u>. I have the new football game.

Tom: I haven't played that one yet. I'll see you soon.

Answer the questions

1. What was John doing when Tom called?
2. How does Tom feel?
3. What is John about to do?
4. Which new video game does John have?

Unscramble the words

1. the / surfing / internet / morning / Tom / been / all / has
2. to / is / shopping / John / go / about
3. Tom / get / John / wants / with / together / to
4. new / game / football / John / the / has

Conversation 2

John: How was the bus ride here?

Tom: It was alright. I used the time to <u>study English</u>.

John: That's a good idea. I haven't started studying yet.

Tom: Who's that <u>playing piano</u> in the living room?

John: That's my cousin, Joe. He's a really good musician.

Tom: Yes, he is. I wish I could play an instrument. I can't even <u>sing songs</u>.

John: Do you want to <u>play video games</u> now?

Tom: Sure. Does Joe want to join us?

John: Only two people can play the football game.

Tom: Perhaps we should <u>play cards</u> instead. Three people can do that.

Answer the questions

1. What was Tom doing on the bus?

2. Who is playing piano in the living room?

3. Why can't Joe play the video game with the two boys?

4. What did Tom suggest to play instead?

Find three nouns, verbs and adjectives

Nouns	Verbs	Adjectives
1. _____	1. _____	2. _____
2. _____	2. _____	2. _____
3. _____	3. _____	3. _____

Take the test

Write the answer next to the letter "A"

A: ___ **1.** What was John doing when Tom called?

a. Playing video games.   b. Watching TV.   c. Surfing the internet.

A: ___ **2.** Why didn't John walk to the library?

a. He's bored.   b. It's raining.   c. He's going shopping.

A: ___ **3.** Tom has ___ surfing the internet all morning.

a. been   b. being   c. be

A: ___ **4.** John is about to ___.

a. play video games   b. go shopping   c. watch TV

A: ___ **5.** Tom took a ___ to John's house.

a. bus   b. train   c. taxi

A: ___ **6.** Tom ___ on the way to John's house.

a. read a book   b. studied English   c. took photographs

A: ___ **7.** They did not play video games because only ___ can play.

a. one person   b. two people   c. three people

A: ___ **8.** The boys decided to invite Joe to play ___.

a. video games   b. piano   c. cards

Answers on Page 206

Lesson 45: Outdoor activities

các hoạt động ngoài trời

Learn the words

1. **kayaking**
   chèo thuyền kayak
2. **going camping**
   đi cắm trại
3. **flying a kite**
   thả diều
4. **riding a horse**
   cưỡi ngựa
5. **going hiking**
   đi bộ đường dài
6. **skydiving**
   nhảy dù
7. **riding a bike**
   đi xe đạp
8. **snowboarding**
   trượt tuyết
9. **going fishing**
   đi câu cá
10. **doing gardening**
    làm vườn

Q&A Pattern 1

What are you doing tomorrow?
I'm planning to go <u>kayaking</u>.

Q&A Pattern 2

Do you mean the place where we <u>go fishing</u>?
No, not there.

Q&A Pattern 3

What do people do here in the winter?
People go <u>snowboarding</u>.

Conversation 1

John: Hi, Tom. It's John. What are you doing tomorrow?

Tom: I'm planning to go kayaking. It's going to be a sunny day.

John: Mom asked me to take Joe out. He would love that.

Tom: I can invite my brother, Brad, to come. He's the same age as Joe.

John: Do you have enough kayaks?

Tom: No, we're going to rent them at the river. We can ride a bike there.

John: Do you mean the place where we go fishing?

Tom: No, not there. Do you remember where we once went camping?

John: Of course, I do. We had a lot of fun that weekend.

Tom: Cool. Let's meet there at ten o'clock in the morning.

Answer the questions

1. What's the weather going to be like tomorrow?

2. What are they planning to do tomorrow?

3. How are they going to get to the river?

4. What time will they meet? _____

Fill in the blanks

John: Hi, Tom. It's _____. What _____ you doing _____?

Tom: I'm _____ to go _____. It's going _____ be a _____ day.

John: Mom _____ me to _____ Joe out. He _____ _____ that.

Tom: I can _____ my _____, Brad, to _____. He's the _____ age as Joe.

Conversation 2

John: Thanks for inviting us to go <u>kayaking</u>. We're both really excited.

Tom: No problem. Was it easy for you to find this place?

John: Yes, it was. Joe and I <u>rode a bike</u> along the river until we found it.

Joe: I know this place well. My sister <u>rides a horse</u> around here in spring.

Tom: It's a popular place to do outdoor activities.

John: That's true. It gets very crowded in the winter.

Joe: What do people do here in the winter?

John: People go <u>snowboarding</u>. The mountain gets a lot of snow.

Tom: We should do that one day. I only <u>go hiking</u> in the mountain.

John: That sounds fun. Let's do it next winter.

Answer the questions

1. What does Joe's sister do in spring?
2. When does the area get crowded?
3. What do people do in winter?
4. What does Tom do in the mountain?

Past or Present?

1. Was it easy for you to find this place? ☐ **Past** ☐ **Present**
2. Joe and I rode a bike along the river until we found it. ☐ **Past** ☐ **Present**
3. My sister rides a horse around here in spring. ☐ **Past** ☐ **Present**
4. The mountain gets a lot of snow. ☐ **Past** ☐ **Present**

Take the test

Write the answer next to the letter "A"

A: ___ **1.** Tom is planning to go ___ tomorrow.

a. kayaking   b. hiking   c. camping

A: ___ **2.** Mom asked John to take ___ out.

a. Brad   b. Joe   c. Tom

A: ___ **3.** Brad and Joe are both ten years old.

a. True.   b. False.   c. Not given.

A: ___ **4.** They are going to meet at the place where they once went ___.

a. fishing   b. riding   c. camping

A: ___ **5.** "Joe and I rode a bike ___ the river until we found it."

a. along   b. around   c. over

A: ___ **6.** Joe's sister ___ a horse around there in spring.

a. ride   b. rides   c. riding

A: ___ **7.** It's a popular place to ___ outdoor activities.

a. do   b. make   c. go

A: ___ **8.** People go ___ on the mountain in the winter.

a. fishing   b. hiking   c. snowboarding

Answers on Page 206

Lesson 46: Ocean life

thế giới đại dương

Learn the words

1. **dolphin** — cá heo
2. **seal** — hải cẩu
3. **whale** — cá voi
4. **octopus** — bạch tuột
5. **shark** — cá mập
6. **jellyfish** — con sứa
7. **tuna** — cá ngừ
8. **salmon** — cá hồi
9. **crab** — cua
10. **squid** — mực ống

Q&A Pattern 1

Did you see any <u>whales</u>?
Yes, I saw a humpback <u>whale</u>.

Q&A Pattern 2

Do <u>sharks</u> visit the area where you were?
Yes, they sometimes do.

Q&A Pattern 3

Are you sure it was an <u>octopus</u>?
Yes, I'm sure it was!

Conversation 1

Helen: How was your trip to Hawaii?

Stan: It was amazing. I had the best time!

Helen: Did you go surfing while you were there?

Stan: Yes, I did. I even saw a <u>dolphin</u> swim by while surfing.

Helen: Wow! You must have been excited to see them.

Stan: At first, I thought it was a <u>shark</u>!

Helen: Luckily, it wasn't one. Do <u>sharks</u> visit the area where you were?

Stan: Yes, they sometimes do. They eat the <u>seals</u> there.

Helen: Did you see any <u>whales</u>?

Stan: Yes, I saw a humpback <u>whale</u>. We went on a <u>whale</u>-watching boat.

Answer the questions

1. How was Stan's trip to Hawaii?
2. What did Stan see while surfing?
3. What do sharks eat in the area?
4. What kind of whale did Stan see?

True or False?

1. Stan enjoyed his time in Hawaii.   ☐ **True** ☐ **False**
2. Stan saw a shark when he went surfing.   ☐ **True** ☐ **False**
3. Sharks eat the seals in the area where Stan was surfing.   ☐ **True** ☐ **False**
4. Stan went whale-watching and saw a beluga whale.   ☐ **True** ☐ **False**

Conversation 2

Helen: I spoke to Stan today about his trip to Hawaii.

Dad: What did he say about it?

Helen: He said he saw a <u>dolphin</u> while surfing.

Joe: That's awesome. The beach near here only has <u>crabs</u>.

Helen: There are also <u>jellyfish</u>, but they're boring to watch.

Joe: It's not a very good beach to see ocean life.

Dad: That's not true. I once saw an <u>octopus</u> in the water.

Joe: Are you sure it was an <u>octopus</u>?

Dad: Yes, I'm sure it was! It was hiding under a rock.

Helen: I think I'd rather see the ocean life in Hawaii.

Answer the questions

1. What does Helen think about watching jellyfish?

2. Does Joe think the beach is a good place to see ocean life?

3. What did Dad see in the water?

4. What was the octopus doing?

Write the prepositions

1. Helen spoke to Stan _____ his trip.

2. The beach _____ their beach has crabs.

3. Dad once saw an octopus _____ the water.

4. The octopus was hiding _____ a rock.

Take the test

Write the answer next to the letter "A"

A: ___ **1.** Stan saw a ___ while surfing.

a. seal	b. shark	c. dolphin

A: ___ **2.** "At first, I thought it ___ a shark!"

a. be	b. is	c. was

A: ___ **3.** Sharks eat ___ in the area.

a. tuna	b. seals	c. salmon

A: ___ **4.** Stan saw a whale when he was ___.

a. surfing	b. on a boat	c. swimming

A: ___ **5.** The beach that Helen and Joe live near only has crabs.

a. True.	b. False.	c. Not given.

A: ___ **6.** Helen thinks ___ are boring to watch.

a. jellyfish	b. octopus	c. crabs

A: ___ **7.** There was an octopus hiding ___ a rock.

a. under	b. behind	c. beside

A: ___ **8.** Which ocean life was not mentioned?

a. Octopus.	b. Squid.	c. Crab.

Answers on Page 206

Lesson 47: In the bathroom

trong nhà tắm

Learn the words

1. **shower**
   vòi hoa sen
2. **bathtub**
   bồn tắm
3. **bath towel**
   khăn tắm
4. **bath mat**
   thảm tắm
5. **mirror**
   gương
6. **toilet**
   phòng vệ sinh
7. **toilet paper**
   giấy vệ sinh
8. **sink**
   bồn rửa
9. **soap**
   xà bông
10. **shelf**
    kệ

Q&A Pattern 1

What do you think of the <u>bathtub</u>?
It's a little small.

Q&A Pattern 2

Are you happy with the <u>shower</u>?
No, I'm not.

Q&A Pattern 3

Is it possible to remove the <u>toilet</u>?
Yes, it can be removed.

Conversation 1

Jill: My bathroom is too old. I want to change it.

Molly: I agree. You have to fix the broken sink.

Jill: I think I'm going to replace it. What do you think of the bathtub?

Molly: It's a little small. There are also a few scratches in it.

Jill: I would love to have a bigger bathtub.

Molly: It might be difficult. The bathroom doesn't have much space.

Jill: I could remove the toilet so that I can put a bigger one in.

Molly: Are you happy with the shower?

Jill: No, I'm not. The water takes a long time to get hot.

Molly: It sounds like you are going to change the whole bathroom!

Answer the questions

1. Does Jill want to fix the sink?
2. What does Molly think about the bathtub?
3. Why is it difficult to put a bigger bathtub in the bathroom?
4. What's wrong with the shower?

Complete the sentences using three words

1. Molly thinks Jill has to fix _____.
2. Jill would love to have _____.
3. The bathroom doesn't _____.
4. It sounds like Jill wants to change _____.

Conversation 2

Thomas: Which part of the bathroom do you want me to change?

Jill: I want to change everything. I also want to put in a bigger bathtub.

Thomas: I don't know how you can do that. There isn't much space.

Jill: Is it possible to remove the toilet?

Thomas: Yes, it can be removed. Where do you want to put it?

Jill: There's a small room next to the bathroom.

Thomas: Okay. We can put it there. You could also remove this big shelf.

Jill: Yes, but I need a shelf in the bathroom.

Thomas: I suggest you put a smaller one under the mirror on the wall.

Jill: That's a great idea. Let's do that!

Answer the questions

1. Where does Jill want to put the toilet?

2. What did Thomas suggest to remove?

3. Does Jill need a shelf in the bathroom?

4. Where will they put a smaller shelf?

Which person?

1. _____ wants to change everything in the bathroom.

2. _____ doesn't know how to put in a bigger bathtub.

3. _____ needs a shelf in the bathroom.

4. _____ suggests to put a small shelf under the mirror.

Take the test

Write the answer next to the letter "A"

A: ___ **1.** Jill wants to change her bathroom because it is too ___.

a. old　　　　　　　　　　b. broken　　　　　　　　　　c. small

A: ___ **2.** Jill is going to fix the bathtub instead of replacing it.

a. True.　　　　　　　　　b. False.　　　　　　　　　　c. Not given.

A: ___ **3.** "The bathroom doesn't have ___ space."

a. many　　　　　　　　　b. a lot　　　　　　　　　　　c. much

A: ___ **4.** The water in the ___ takes too long to get hot.

a. bathtub　　　　　　　　b. shower　　　　　　　　　　c. sink

A: ___ **5.** What will be removed from the bathroom?

a. The bathtub.　　　　　　b. The toilet.　　　　　　　　c. The shower.

A: ___ **6.** Thomas doesn't know ___ to put a bigger bathtub in the bathroom.

a. how　　　　　　　　　　b. what　　　　　　　　　　　c. why

A: ___ **7.** Jill needs a ___ in the bathroom.

a. bath towel　　　　　　　b. bath mat　　　　　　　　　c. shelf

A: ___ **8.** A smaller shelf will be put ___ the mirror.

a. across from　　　　　　 b. above　　　　　　　　　　c. under

Answers on Page 206

Lesson 48: Capital cities

thành phố thủ đô

Learn the words

1. **London**
   London
2. **Madrid**
   Madrid
3. **Paris**
   Paris
4. **Ottawa**
   Ottawa
5. **Washington, D.C.**
   Washington, D.C
6. **Cape Town**
   Thị trấn Cape
7. **Wellington**
   Wellington
8. **Canberra**
   Canberra
9. **Bangkok**
   Băng cốc
10. **Beijing**
    Bắc Kinh

Q&A Pattern 1

Can you take me to <u>Washington, D.C.</u> this Friday?
No, I can't.

Q&A Pattern 2

In which city does she live?
She lives in <u>Canberra</u>.

Q&A Pattern 3

Is <u>Bangkok</u> the capital city of Thailand?
Yes, that's right.

Conversation 1

Helen: Can you take me to Washington, D.C. this Friday?

Dad: No, I can't. I have a business meeting in Ottawa this week.

Mom: Why do you need to go to Washington, D.C.?

Helen: My classmate from New Zealand wants to see the capital city.

Dad: New Zealand is a beautiful country.

Helen: Stacy was born in Wellington, but actually lives in Australia.

Mom: In which city does she live?

Helen: She lives in Canberra.

Mom: That's very far from here. Did her family come over as well?

Helen: No, they didn't. She's an exchange student here.

Answer the questions

1. When does Helen need to go to Washington, D.C.?

2. Why can't Dad take Helen to Washington, D.C.?

3. What does Dad think about New Zealand?

4. Where was Stacy born?

Put the sentences in order

Dad has a meeting in Ottawa. ___

Helen wants Dad to take her to Washington, D.C. this Friday. (1)

Stacy's family didn't come with her because she's an exchange student. ___

Helen's classmate was born in New Zealand. ___

Conversation 2

Mom: Why do you have to go to Ottawa for a business meeting?

Dad: The company wants to open an office in Asia.

Mom: Which city are they thinking about opening one in?

Dad: They're still discussing it. I'm hoping they choose Thailand's capital.

Mom: Is Bangkok the capital city of Thailand?

Dad: Yes, that's right. They are also considering Beijing.

Mom: Why do you want them to choose Thailand?

Dad: Both cities are great. I love Thai food, so I hope Bangkok is chosen.

Mom: Once they've chosen a city, will you have to go?

Dad: Yes, I will go there to help set the office up. You can come if you like.

Answer the questions

1. Which two cities is the company considering opening an office in?

2. What is the capital city of Thailand?

3. Why does Dad hope the company chooses Bangkok?

4. What will Dad do once they've chosen a city?

Noun, Verb or Adjective?

open ☐ Noun ☐ Verb ☐ ADJ

cities ☐ Noun ☐ Verb ☐ ADJ

office ☐ Noun ☐ Verb ☐ ADJ

considering ☐ Noun ☐ Verb ☐ ADJ

great ☐ Noun ☐ Verb ☐ ADJ

hope ☐ Noun ☐ Verb ☐ ADJ

company ☐ Noun ☐ Verb ☐ ADJ

right ☐ Noun ☐ Verb ☐ ADJ

Take the test

Write the answer next to the letter "A"

A: ___ **1.** Dad has a meeting in ___ this week.

a. Washington, D.C. b. Ottawa c. Wellington

A: ___ **2.** Dad thinks ___ is a beautiful country.

a. Thailand b. Australia c. New Zealand

A: ___ **3.** Helen's classmate was born in Canberra, but actually lives in New Zealand.

a. True. b. False. c. Not given.

A: ___ **4.** Stacy's family didn't ___ her.

a. come for b. come to c. come with

A: ___ **5.** In which city did the company choose to open an office in?

a. They haven't chosen one. b. Beijing. c. Bangkok.

A: ___ **6.** What is the capital city of Thailand?

a. Beijing. b. Bangkok. c. Canberra.

A: ___ **7.** "I love Thai food, so I hope Bangkok is ___."

a. choosing b. chosen c. chose

A: ___ **8.** Dad will go to the new office in Asia to help ___ it up.

a. set b. put c. prepare

Answers on Page 206

Lesson 49: In the toolbox

trong hộp công cụ

Learn the words

1. **a hammer**
   cây búa
2. **a shovel**
   xẻng
3. **a paintbrush**
   cọ sơn
4. **a screwdriver**
   cái vặn vít
5. **an electric drill**
   máy khoan điện
6. **a tape measure**
   thước dây
7. **a wrench**
   cờ lê
8. **a ladder**
   thang
9. **pliers**
   kìm
10. **an axe**
    rìu

Q&A Pattern 1

Which tool do you need to use first?
I need to use the screwdriver first.

Q&A Pattern 2

Where is the tape measure?
It should be in the toolbox.

Q&A Pattern 3

Can you fix that part of the gate?
No, I don't think so.

Conversation 1

Mom: Before you leave for Ottawa, can you please fix the gate?

Dad: Yes, I'll do that right away. Joe can help me.

Joe: Okay. I'll go and get the toolbox.

Dad: Bring the small <u>ladder</u>, too. The gate is quite high.

Joe: Which tool do you need to use first?

Dad: I need to use the <u>screwdriver</u> first.

Joe: Are you sure you don't want to use the <u>electric drill</u> instead?

Dad: These screws are old. I might need to pull them out with a <u>hammer</u>.

Joe: There are holes in the wood. Can you fix that part of the gate?

Dad: No, I don't think so. This part of the gate needs replacing.

Answer the questions

1. What does Mom want Dad to fix?
2. Why does Dad want the small ladder?
3. Which tool did Dad want to use first?
4. Why can't Dad take out the screws with a screwdriver?

Unscramble the words

1. fix / Dad / wants / gate / Mom / the / to
2. the / will / toolbox / Joe / get
3. to / first / Dad / screwdriver / the / use / needs
4. in / wood / the / There / holes / are

Conversation 2

Dad: Joe and I are going to the hardware store.

Mom: Why? Is there something wrong?

Dad: Some of the wood needs replacing. I'll need to buy some material.

Joe: Should we measure the size of the wood first?

Dad: Yes, we should. Hand me the <u>tape measure</u>.

Joe: It's not in the toolbox. Where is the <u>tape measure</u>?

Dad: It should be in the toolbox. Check under the <u>pliers</u>.

Joe: It's not here. I think Mom was using it when she was painting the chairs.

Mom: Yes, I forgot to put it back. It's in the box where I put the <u>paintbrushes</u>.

Dad: I might also buy a new <u>axe</u> so that I can chop up the old wood.

Answer the questions

1. Where are Dad and Joe going?

2. Is the tape measure under the pliers?

3. Where did Mom put the tape measure?

4. Which tool does Dad want to buy?

Find three nouns, verbs and adjectives

Nouns

1. _____

2. _____

3. _____

Verbs

1. _____

2. _____

3. _____

Adjectives

2. _____

2. _____

3. _____

Take the test

Write the answer next to the letter "A"

A: ___ **1.** Mom wants Dad to fix the ___.

a. fence b. door c. gate

A: ___ **2.** Dad needs a ladder because the gate ___.

a. is high b. is broken c. needs replacing

A: ___ **3.** What will Dad use to pull out the screws?

a. A screwdriver. b. An electric drill. c. A hammer.

A: ___ **4.** A part of the gate needs replacing because ___.

a. it is too high b. the wood has holes c. the screws are old

A: ___ **5.** The boys are going to the department store to get ___.

a. some screws b. a tape measure c. some material

A: ___ **6.** Mom put the tape measure ___.

a. under the pliers b. in a box with paintbrushes c. in the toolbox

A: ___ **7.** Dad will buy a new ___ to chop up the old wood.

a. hammer b. wrench c. axe

A: ___ **8.** Which tool was not mentioned?

a. The ladder. b. The shovel. c. The electric drill.

Answers on Page 206

Lesson 50: At the cinema

ở rạp chiếu phim

Learn the words

1. exciting
   thú vị
2. scary
   đáng sợ
3. romantic
   lãng mạn
4. violent
   hung bạo
5. informative
   nhiều thông tin
6. interesting
   hấp dẫn
7. boring
   nhàm chán
8. enjoyable
   thú vị
9. sad
   buồn
10. funny
    buồn cười

Q&A Pattern 1

Do you want to go to the cinema with me tonight?
Yes, I do if there's an <u>interesting</u> movie on.

Q&A Pattern 2

What kind of movie would you like to watch?
I'd like to see a <u>funny</u> one.

Q&A Pattern 3

What did you think of the movie?
I thought it was a little <u>violent</u>.

Conversation 1

Sally: Do you want to go to the cinema with me tonight?

Candice: Yes, I do if there's an interesting movie on.

Sally: I've got the movie timetable here. *Fridays at Fran's* starts today.

Candice: I heard it's really scary. I'm not sure I want to see a horror movie.

Sally: What kind of movie would you like to watch?

Candice: I'd like to see a funny one. It would be nice to laugh.

Sally: Yes, that would be more enjoyable.

Candice: If there isn't a good comedy, we could see something else.

Sally: There's a new superhero movie on right now.

Candice: That could be exciting. Let's see that one.

Answer the questions

1. What are the girls going to do tonight?

2. Why didn't Candice want to see the movie, *Fridays at Fran's*?

3. Who wants to see a movie that makes them laugh?

4. What kind of movie did they decide to see?

Fill in the blanks

Sally: What _____ of _____ would you _____ to _____?

Candice: I'd _____ to see a _____ one. It _____ be nice to _____.

Sally: Yes, that _____ _____ more _____.

Candice: If _____ _____ a good _____, we could see _____ else.

Conversation 2

Candice: What did you think of the movie?

Sally: I thought it was a little <u>violent</u>.

Candice: That's true, but it was also <u>funny</u> at times.

Sally: I laughed a lot at Peter's best friend. He's also a good actor.

Candice: I was surprised how <u>interesting</u> the storyline was.

Sally: I agree. Usually, the storylines in superhero movies are quite <u>boring</u>.

Candice: It was <u>sad</u> when the uncle died.

Sally: I agree. I was shocked when that happened.

Candice: What did you think of the girl who Peter liked?

Sally: I thought she was cute. It was <u>romantic</u> when she first spoke to Peter.

Answer the questions

1. Who thought the movie was too violent?

2. What was Candace surprised by?

3. What does Sally usually think of superhero movies?

4. What did Sally find romantic?

Past or Present?

1. I laughed a lot at Peter's best friend. ☐ **Past** ☐ **Present**

2. The storylines in superhero movies are quite boring. ☐ **Past** ☐ **Present**

3. He's also a good actor. ☐ **Past** ☐ **Present**

4. It was sad when the uncle died. ☐ **Past** ☐ **Present**

Take the test

Write the answer next to the letter "A"

A: ___ **1.** Candice doesn't want to see *Fridays at Fran's* because she heard it's ___.

a. violent   b. scary   c. boring

A: ___ **2.** Candice wanted to see a ___ movie at first.

a. exciting   b. funny   c. romantic

A: ___ **3.** "If there isn't a good comedy, we could see something ___."

a. other   b. otherwise   c. else

A: ___ **4.** The girls finally decided to see ___ movie.

a. an informative   b. a superhero   c. a funny

A: ___ **5.** The movie was a little violent, but it was also funny.

a. True.   b. False.   c. Not given.

A: ___ **6.** Sally thinks the storylines in superhero movies are usually ___.

a. violent   b. funny   c. boring

A: ___ **7.** Sally was ___ when the uncle in the movie died.

a. shock   b. shocked   c. shocking

A: ___ **8.** Sally thought it was ___ when the girl first spoke with Peter.

a. romantic   b. interesting   c. funny

Answers on Page 206

Answers

Test 1-5	Lesson 1	Lesson 2	Lesson 3	Lesson 4	Lesson 5
Question 1	b	c	a	c	c
Question 2	a	b	c	b	b
Question 3	c	c	a	a	b
Question 4	a	b	c	a	c
Question 5	c	a	b	a	c
Question 6	b	b	b	c	b
Question 7	c	b	c	b	b
Question 8	a	a	a	b	c

Test 6-10	Lesson 6	Lesson 7	Lesson 8	Lesson 9	Lesson 10
Question 1	a	c	b	b	c
Question 2	b	b	c	b	a
Question 3	a	c	a	c	c
Question 4	b	a	c	b	c
Question 5	b	c	b	c	a
Question 6	b	b	b	a	a
Question 7	c	b	a	c	b
Question 8	b	c	a	b	c

Test 11-15	Lesson 11	Lesson 12	Lesson 13	Lesson 14	Lesson 15
Question 1	c	b	a	b	b
Question 2	b	c	b	c	c
Question 3	b	b	c	b	a
Question 4	c	a	a	a	c
Question 5	b	c	c	c	b
Question 6	a	a	c	b	c
Question 7	b	b	b	a	b
Question 8	a	c	a	b	b

Test 16-20	Lesson 16	Lesson 17	Lesson 18	Lesson 19	Lesson 20
Question 1	a	a	c	c	a
Question 2	b	b	c	c	b
Question 3	c	a	b	b	c
Question 4	b	b	c	c	b
Question 5	a	c	c	a	b
Question 6	b	c	a	b	b
Question 7	b	b	b	c	a
Question 8	c	a	c	b	c

Test 21-25	Lesson 21	Lesson 22	Lesson 23	Lesson 24	Lesson 25
Question 1	c	b	c	a	c
Question 2	b	c	b	a	b
Question 3	c	b	b	c	b
Question 4	c	a	a	c	a
Question 5	b	b	b	b	b
Question 6	a	c	c	a	a
Question 7	c	b	b	c	c
Question 8	a	a	b	a	c

Test 26-30	Lesson 26	Lesson 27	Lesson 28	Lesson 29	Lesson 30
Question 1	b	a	b	c	b
Question 2	c	b	c	b	b
Question 3	a	a	a	a	a
Question 4	b	b	b	c	c
Question 5	a	c	a	a	b
Question 6	a	a	b	a	c
Question 7	c	c	c	c	c
Question 8	b	c	b	b	a

Test 31-35	Lesson 31	Lesson 32	Lesson 33	Lesson 34	Lesson 35
Question 1	c	c	c	b	a
Question 2	b	b	b	c	c
Question 3	a	b	b	b	c
Question 4	b	c	a	a	a
Question 5	b	a	a	c	b
Question 6	c	c	b	b	b
Question 7	b	b	b	a	c
Question 8	a	c	c	b	b

Test 36-40	Lesson 36	Lesson 37	Lesson 38	Lesson 39	Lesson 40
Question 1	a	b	b	c	b
Question 2	a	a	b	b	c
Question 3	b	b	c	c	b
Question 4	c	b	b	a	a
Question 5	b	c	b	b	c
Question 6	a	c	a	a	b
Question 7	c	b	c	a	a
Question 8	a	c	a	b	a

Test 41-45	Lesson 41	Lesson 42	Lesson 43	Lesson 44	Lesson 45
Question 1	b	a	c	b	a
Question 2	c	a	a	b	b
Question 3	c	b	c	a	c
Question 4	b	c	b	b	c
Question 5	b	c	c	a	a
Question 6	a	b	b	b	b
Question 7	c	a	a	b	a
Question 8	a	b	c	c	c

Test 46-50	Lesson 46	Lesson 47	Lesson 48	Lesson 49	Lesson 50
Question 1	c	a	b	c	b
Question 2	c	b	c	a	b
Question 3	b	c	b	c	c
Question 4	b	b	c	b	b
Question 5	b	b	a	c	a
Question 6	a	a	b	b	c
Question 7	a	c	b	c	b
Question 8	b	c	a	b	a

Milton Keynes UK
Ingram Content Group UK Ltd.
UKHW032259291123
433514UK00004B/67